BEYOND FORGIVENESS
MY TRUE LIFE STORY

The strength of my soul was born
on the backs of moments that
brought me to my knees.

CONTENTS

Introduction 7

1. 1947. Copenhagen 10

2. 1950. We Arrive Back In Copenhagen 14

3. 1957. I Get Yet Another New Father 20

4. 1959. A New Life Begins On Our Own 26

5. 1961. A New Life Begins In England 31

6. 1962. I Turn To God For Help 39

7. 1965. My Last Days At School 44

8. 1967. My Marrage To Piers 50

9. 1969. Filming In New York 54

10. 1970. My Time With Roman Polanski 58

11. 1972. Off To Australia 68

12. 1974. I Meet The Dutchman 72

13. 1974. Back In Australia 82

14. 1975. Back To England 84

15. 1975. Back In Rome 86

16. 1975. Natasha Is Born 88

17. 1976. Life Begins In England Again 92

18. 1982. A New Life Begins In London 100

19. 1985. Who Am I? 104

20. 1988. Take Robert To Court 108

21. 1990. Another Big Trauma 112

22. 1993. Reiki And Healing Enters My Life 115

23. 1994. A Difficult Meeting 121

24. 1994. Meeting Jack Temple 123

25. 1995. Enter The Royal Family 131

26. 1996. Enter Princess Diana Into My Life 136

27. 1995. Enter Sri Sathya Sai Baba 144

28. 1996. My Meeting With Kaya Günata 149

29. 1997. More About Princess Diana 156

30. 1997. My First Meeting With Dolphins 160

31. 1997. A New Life Begins In Florida 171

32. 1998. I Set Up My Own Dolphin Healing Centre 177

33. 1998. Enter My American Husband -
To Be Or Not To Be! 180

34. 1999. Back To India For Answers 188

35. 2000. I Move Back To England 198

36. 2003. My Calling To Become An Inter-Faith Minister ... 208

37. August 2005. My Ordination 218

38. 2006. Life In Moat Hall Begins ~
15 Years In Loving Service 222

39. 2010. Another Visit To Sai Baba's Ashram 227

40. 2012. A Turning Point 238

41. 2014. Enter Sadguru Madhusudan Sai - Sathya Sai
Grama Muddenahalli Ashram, Bangalore, India 244

Epilogue 291

Conclusion 296

Why Share Personal Experiences? And How? 299

The Law Of Surrender And Detatchment 305

Tools For Self-Help 307

More On Sai Baba 308

INTRODUCTION

The Bhagavad-Gita, the ancient Indian Holy Book, says it is better to live your own destiny imperfectly, than to live an imitation of someone else's life with perfection.

Our painful experiences aren't a liability – they are a gift. They give us perspective and meaning, an opportunity to find our unique purpose, our strength, and our opportunities for growth. We hold the key to our own freedom. Freedom lies in learning to embrace what happened. It is easier to hold someone or something else responsible for our pain, than to take responsibility for ending our own victimhood. No one can make you a victim. Therefore, ask yourself, instead of "Why me?", "Why not me?"

Memory is sacred ground, therefore I am bringing the value of my lived experiences to the arena, so that I can then feel an authentic sense of fulfilment, that all my life's ups and downs have been for a purpose, but more importantly, for anyone else who is struggling with their own self-worth, that they might gain hope and strength to live their best life.

There *is* life after trauma, life after rejection, after

lies, after loss, after betrayal, after abuse, after failure and after heartbreaks.

You can still create a beautiful, happy and peaceful life for yourself, even if you are broken. That heartbeat in your chest is a sign of hope.

Your traumas do not define the rest of your life. There is still a possibility for new beginnings.

We don't want to shrink and disappear into oblivion. We want to recognize who we are. Our character is unique. Our Atman is universal. We are not born average, normal or typical, or a carbon copy. We are born unique. Born to manifest the glory of the universe in our own authentic, most passionate way. We are stronger than we imagine, wiser than we know and have vast powers that have yet to be actualized.

To see and understand our predicaments clearly is a first step in going,

BEYOND FORGIVENESS.

What would have become of me if I had not heard Your call?

In 1997, I took Sarah, Duchess of York, to India to meet my Spiritual Teacher, Sri Sathya Sai Baba. He told me then, whilst patting my shoulder, "Very good woman, but sometimes a little mad!" It is this goodness and madness I will now attempt to write about. My hope and prayer is that it will give inspiration to the reader, to rise above any traumatic experiences or dramas they may have gone through in their life, therefore through self-enquiry, find peace and salvation.

I want to turn to the inherent goodness that lies within each of us, making our life into a magnificent song, in tune with the Beloved. If we remember we are not the body, that our mind and our personality is just a tool to negotiate life, remembering instead that we are divine beings, having experiences that our soul calls forth, then we will be able to get through every aspect of life. If this book helps just one person, it will have been worth writing it.

Of course, it was potentially completely 'mad' in the first place to come into this world the way I did. I chose a beautiful mother, who was often mistaken for being Ingrid Bergman, who fell in love with a forbidden person.

I suppose another reason I am writing this book is that I have to prove to myself that my birth was not a mistake; that after all the ups and downs experienced, I have eventually tried to make the best of this chance called life, especially now that I have realized the only free will we have is to choose to identify with our bodies as the totality of who we are, or choose who we really are: eternal God beings.

My Mother 1947

CHAPTER 1

1947. COPENHAGEN

Apparently, I was conceived in a church. Now that really appeals to me. It might not appeal to a lot of people out there though. Sinful, disrespectful, etc., comes to mind. But is it? If God had *not* wanted me to be conceived in a church, would it have happened? Especially as the two people concerned were really good God-loving people themselves.

My parents were in love, there was no doubt about that. They were both in loveless marriages and hungry for love. My father had been on the front line during most of the war, giving the last rights to the dying soldiers as Chaplain to the Forces at Slesvig in Germany. The cross he used for this purpose I now have as my only possession of his. My mother was married to a wealthy Danish businessman. They had married in Copenhagen, just before the war. My mother realized very early on in her marriage that she had made a dreadful mistake. But as she got pregnant soon after with my eldest sister, she decided to give it a go.

As time went by, my mother asked for a separation. Her husband pleaded with her after a while to come back to him, enticing her with the news that the new vicar to the English church was looking for more good singers for the choir. Queen Elizabeth II was coming for a visit and always came to the English Church, if her schedule allowed it.

My mother came back to give her marriage a second try, but instead fell in love, over a period of time, with the charismatic vicar!

A strong romance started. Secret meetings began for these forbidden lovers. One day, their passion surpassed their good sense and they made love somewhere in the church.

When my mother found out she was pregnant with me, she told my father, who immediately said they should get married.

My parents desperately wanted to get married, but the then Archbishop of Canterbury, Geoffrey Francis Fisher, refused their request.

In fact, the archbishop told my father to forget about "*that woman and her child*" and forbade my father to have any further contact with us. He was sent back to England into exile for a while.

It is only recently I have come to realize that my father's love for God was stronger than his love or duty to my mother or myself. You may think this sounds bizarre, but I feel totally comfortable with this. You see, I am in love with God myself.

So, my father stayed with his wife, but my mother separated from her husband and moved away from Copenhagen to a tiny cottage in Wales, England, with my older half-sister. She said a brief goodbye to her parents before setting off on her lonely journey. I cannot imagine how my mother must have felt leaving everything behind and journeying alone to a foreign place. I have been back there and know it was not by chance that my mother chose this spot for me to be born. It is a magnificent, holy place. She had pressed so sharply against life and was hurting. Here she could spend the rest of her pregnancy contemplating the beautiful nature all around her. Stepping into silence was her salvation. She loved this time of her life, and so did my half-sister. In fact, when my sister had to return to Copenhagen, to spend the summer holidays with her father, and was subsequently not returned to my mother, my sister was traumatised.

After nearly two years of blissful living, my mother was running out of funds, therefore needed to find work. Before she was married, she had trained as a nurse. She found a job in a hospital in Ascot and put me into a children's home. After a few weeks, the matron of the home called my mother, informing her that if she did not come and fetch me, I would die, as I was not eating. Apparently, I was not unhappy or crying, just sitting in a corner crossed-legged, smiling but not eating; probably the youngest known person who ever went on hunger strike! My sister, who was living with her father by now, was pining dreadfully for my mother, therefore mother decided to pick me up and we moved back to Copenhagen. So began a new life.

Me age 3

CHAPTER 2

1950. WE ARRIVE BACK IN COPENHAGEN

My mother's husband was astounded to see her arrive with a small child in her arms. She told him the truth and was finally granted a divorce! Several months of hardship followed. My posh grandparents were not at all amused by this turn of events and did little to help.

I GET A NEW FATHER

After a while, whilst staying with friends, my mother applied for a job with a well-known lawyer, who was

Left: My Far 1951. Right: Christmas Eve 1952

divorced, to look after his daughter. She got the job immediately and we settled in nicely. I was two years old.

Eventually, my mother succumbed and married this wonderful, good-looking man, whom I grew up believing was my own father. A few years passed, and my younger sister was born. I was thrilled and adored her. I remember the early part of my childhood as being idyllic. I was a happy child and adored both my mother and supposed father. My father called me his "little lion", and I felt that he loved me deeply, as I loved him back.

At the age of 9, I had my first mystical experience

when the whole family were on holiday in Norway. My dad had helped me build a small hut, made of pine branches, by a babbling stream. We decked the ground inside with moss. I then asked him to leave me to be by myself. I sat there for hours, getting intoxicated on pine needles and the sound of the water running gently across the stones in the stream. It felt so peaceful and special that the memory is still fresh in my mind, transporting me back to the moment when I knew for certain that I was in the presence of something magnificent that I could tap into whenever I needed to.

At the age of 10, I was asked to model at the top fashion store Fonsbeck in Copenhagen. I decided then and there that I wanted to become a model when I grew up! It was magical growing up in Copenhagen, especially around Christmas time. I think this is why I adore Christmas. I can't get the Christmas decorations up soon enough. All kinds of wonderful endearing memories come flooding back when I think of Christmas. This is where my mother excelled. She loved Christmas herself and made it special.

On Christmas eve, which is when Christmas is celebrated in Denmark, we would all march off to church around 5pm, the snow glistening in the dark, as if a million diamonds had been thrown from the sky. The church was lit with live candles, the service was always sweet and poignant. After it was finished, we would run back through the snow, anticipating a wonderful meal that our mother and cook had been preparing in our absence.

We were never disappointed, as when we all came through the front door, the smell of goose and red cabbage accosted our nostrils. After washing our hands, we were led into the dining room, with the table beautifully decorated by my mother. Soon we were all tucking into the most delicious meal. Inevitably, some red wine would be spilt, then grandfather (on my mother's side) would shout for the salt so it could be piled on the red spill. It was always a jolly atmosphere, but the anticipation of leaving the dining room and being led into the sitting room was almost too much for us youngsters. After our meal, always finished off with some Lubecker marzipan, my favourite, we would all leave the table and stand in silence in the hall, while my mother disappeared for a moment.

Then the doors to the sitting room would be reverently opened. There in all its splendour would be the big Christmas tree, so beautifully decorated in secret by our mother. The live candles would be glowing on the tree, as well as an abundant of presents underneath. There was always a bucket of water in the corner of the room in case the live tree should catch fire! First, we all gathered around the tree, holding hands, singing Christmas carols. I enjoyed this a lot but often got rather overexcited thinking about what presents I might receive after the joy of singing. I think one of my best Christmases was when I was given a beautiful doll and a real pram I could use outside. I had a passion for playing with dolls when I was young and can still feel the joy it gave me. Whenever I was sick in bed with a chest infection, which was often, I would ask for a shoe box and would make it into a house, with curtains, carpets and little dolls, making up a family. I think these were early signs of wanting to be a homemaker.

During the summer months, we would all get on our bikes and ride into the woods. When I was very little, I remember sitting in a special chair on the back of my dad's bicycle. I would always ask him to go faster. I can still remember him saying, "My little lion, you are fearless." During the summer, we would also take our annual holiday on Fanø island, where we would spend endless hours looking for amber by the water's edge and searching for gull's eggs in the dunes.

In autumn, we would again jump on our bikes and go hunting for blackberries, bringing the berries back to the kitchen to be made into jam, my dad's speciality.

But apparently all was not going well between

my parents. My dad, who was a handsome lawyer, was prone to having affairs with other beautiful women. At age 10, whilst having lunch one day alone with my mother and little sister, my mother asked me if I wanted a new daddy. I was speechless to say the least and nearly choaked on my mouthful of food. I told her I did not, as I was quite happy with the one I had. She then said, "Oh, did I not tell you that your *real* father is dead?" My whole world crashed around my head for a couple of hours. Just like the trooper I am, I picked myself up, dusted myself down and started all over again. This was when I moved into the energy of that "something magnificent" that manages to sustain me.

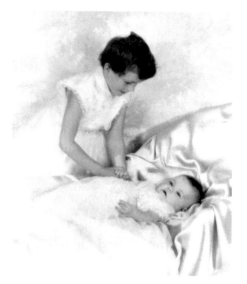

My little sisters Christening 1955

Our new home in Gentofte 1958

CHAPTER 3

1957. I GET YET ANOTHER NEW FATHER

As my mother was to marry a doctor to the Royal Danish family, she managed to get divorced in one week and married the next. Before I could take a deep breath, we moved from our lovely cosy house in Ordrop into a huge house just outside Copenhagen by Gentofte hospital, with two nannies and other staff. I must confess, I liked my new daddy "Tony" quite a lot on our first meeting. He was older than my previous daddy and had kind, intelligent eyes. He made me feel very comfortable in our new home. I still don't quite understand how I managed to adjust so quickly to my new life; I missed my old daddy a lot and used to have dreams about him, sometimes finding my pillow wet with tears when I woke up in the morning.

My new father legally adopted me, and I was given his surname. As the French convent school was closer to our new home, I attended there for a while. But I missed my friends at my old school, so asked if I could return there. It was a long bus ride or cycle ride in the summer, but I was happy to be back amongst friends. I remember when I started there again and the register was read out with my new surname; how strange I felt when everyone stared at me and started asking questions. But I got used to it pretty quickly. That's me. I get used to strange situations at an alarmingly fast rate. I did love my school so much and was happy to be back there. I had plenty of friends and got much attention from teachers.

Whilst my mother and her new husband were away on their honeymoon, one day, the front doorbell rang just as I was walking past it. I had been given strict instructions *not* to open the front door to anyone. But no staff seemed to have heard it, so, when it rang again, loud and persistent, I decided to do the one thing I was *not* supposed to do. As I opened the front door, I saw, standing in the rain, a man with a big box in his hands. He asked me in a very polite tone if my father was in. I told him "No." "Is your mother in?" asked the man. I again replied, "No." He then proceeded to tell me that he had a box of wine for my father. I politely informed him that the tradesman's entrance was to the right of the house and down the stairs. Rudely, I thought, he barged past me and plonked the case down in the entrance hall, announcing, "Tell your father that Prince Knud has personally delivered a box of wine for him." I don't remember saying a word as I saw the Crown Prince of Denmark disappearing down the steps and getting into his car. My new father had recently saved the prince's life after performing a serious operation on him, hence the gift of wine that was personally delivered.

Life in our new home was very grand. Soon after my parents came back from their honeymoon, there was a big party held at our house, with the Danish Royal Family as main guests. For days our cook was busy in the kitchen, preparing the special dinner. I watched her getting redder and redder in the face as the days went by, a bad temper adding to the bargain. Mother was very pre-occupied as well, so this gave me plenty of time to think up a plan of how to avoid attending the presentation to the Royals, which my sisters and I were deemed to attend. You see, I was not a bit interested in coming face to face with His Royal Highness Crown Prince Knud again.

The dreaded day arrived, and I woke up feeling sick. I wasn't actually sick, but I felt it. Could I induce a fever so as to stay in bed? No I could not, even though I tried jolly hard. So the time came when our nannies got us three girls dressed up in our beautiful dresses, white socks and party shoes. To this day, I still remember coming down the circular staircase, shaking like a leaf. Nanny, of course, thought I was nervous. I was, but not for the reason she suspected.

As we entered the drawing room, the guests were sitting in a moon-shaped circle. Mother proudly introduced us to the King and Queen, and then came the dreaded moment when I was being introduced to Prince Knud. I curtsied, looking down at my shoes. I truly felt as if I was about to faint. What if, in a loud voice, in front of all the guests and my parents, the Prince announced that I had tried to send him down the tradesmen's entrance?

My mother was tugging at my hand, and as I looked up at her, she mouthed, "What is the matter?"

The kind Prince came to my rescue, asking me what my most favourite sweet was. I said in a low whisper, "Lubecker Marzipan."

The following day, after a resounding success for my mother and cook, several large bouquets of flowers arrived, as well as a packet from Prince Knud for me! My parents were very intrigued as to why a packet addressed to me had arrived from the palace. I opened it and found the biggest piece of Lubecker Marzipan I'd ever seen and have ever seen since. It was all a big mystery for everyone, but I was thrilled that my secret was safe with the Prince.

It was during this time that I was chosen to play the Virgin Mary in our Christmas school play. I think this sowed the seed for me to want to become an actress. But my Mother used to always say to me, "Nobody in our family are from the acting world, so I don't see how you think you can become an actress!"

Soon after my mother's new marriage, she became ill and had to have a serious operation. She left for Spain to recuperate in the sun. One evening, daddy Tony called me into his bedroom, where he was lying on his bed. He asked me to sit down and told me he was going away for the weekend, as he had recently been working very hard and needed a rest. He told me I was a good girl and to make sure I looked after myself. The following morning, he came to say goodbye to me again. With tears in his eyes, he told me to be a good girl and understand that I could go far in life if I put my mind to it and did not listen to what my mother had to say about that topic. My inner being sensed that something wasn't quite right in his tired expression, so I gave him a big hug and told him to come back soon.

A few days later, the police were knocking on our front door, asking for my mother. They were told she was abroad, so nanny spoke to them instead. I shall never forget the look on her face when she came into the nursery, where I was sitting doing my school homework. The colour had drained from her face, and she was shaking. She told me that she was unable to tell me anything and to get on with my homework.

The next morning, I was about to get ready for school when I bumped into my grandmother coming out of the guest bedroom. She informed me that I would not be going to school as there had been a dreadful incident. Daddy Tony was dead! I was shocked. Having been the last person to see and speak to him, I felt sure it was my fault he was dead, as I had told no one of our conversation or him feeling tired.

The next day, my mother arrived from Spain. She was all dressed in black, and I could see she had been crying a lot. I don't remember what happened during the next few days, but the house was so quiet. No one was smiling, and such sadness hung in the air.

CHAPTER 4

1959. A NEW LIFE BEGINS ON OUR OWN

The day came when we had to leave the big house and move into a smaller one. Only one nanny came with us. We were very fortunate to have inherited some beautiful antique furniture, art and paintings, as well as a lot of money. Our new home looked very imposing. My mother seemed to be alright, and life resumed its normal daily activities.

One day, I was at school when one of my girlfriends, whose father was head of police, told me that my adopted father had committed suicide. I was horrified. When I got back from school, I told my older sister what my girlfriend had said but made her promise not to say a word about it to our mother, as it would make her very upset. I could not bear to see my mother sad, as she had only recently started smiling again.

I had just climbed into my bed for the night

when my mother entered my bedroom. I could see she was looking thoughtful. She sat on my bed and said she wanted to talk to me. After a few moments of silence, she took my hand and said, "Darling, I know you asked your sister not to tell me what your girlfriend told you at school today about Daddy Tony, but it is true!"

I felt cold all over. Mind you, I was only 12 years old, and I don't even think I knew exactly what suicide meant. In those days, we did not have television and childhood was supposedly lived in blissful ignorance. I finally managed to find my voice and asked, how, why? She told me that he was suffering from cancer of the bowels. He had not wanted for us to see him die a dreadful death, so he had done a very courageous thing by taking his own life.

Many years later, I found out that he had gone to a hotel in Copenhagen after our last goodbye, went to see the opera "Madame Butterfly", then gone back to his hotel room, giving himself a lethal injection. Years later I found in my mother's processions after her death a note she had written. It was clear that her mind had started to find it increasingly difficult to cope with life's blows. The note said that it was probably my fault that he had committed suicide, as I must have told him that she was still in love with my father!

So, back to that extraordinary night, with my mother sitting on my bed, telling me that Daddy Tony had committed suicide. After a while, she looked at me and asked in a strange voice, "Darling, can you take something else?" What a funny question! I must have said yes, because with the next breath she said to me, "You remember I told you that your real father was dead? Well, he isn't. He is alive. I just wanted to tell you now before you hear it from anyone else."

Right now, right this minute, as I am sitting at my computer, writing this down, I have been still for quite a long time. I feel a bit shaky, as if I haven't properly let myself feel that moment of revelation before. If I was a smoker, I might reach for a cigarette, but I am not a smoker. I might get a glass of wine, but I am not a drinker. So I am just going to take a bit of time out. I will be back shortly.

I am back! But I have a very big confession to make. After sitting for a while on my sofa, not really wanting or willing to get in touch with that moment in my life, I went searching for a bottle of wine. I found an old dusty bottle that someone must have given me years ago. I have opened it and taken a sip. It tastes quite nice! In fact, it feels very grown up, drinking this glass of dusty old wine. I need to feel grown up right now. I don't want to be that 12-year-old girl, sitting in her bed feeling very confused. I just want to be NORMAL. I don't want to feel like an outsider.

I especially did not want to remember the next words my mother told me. "Darling, this is our secret. Never tell anyone this story, because no one will ever want to marry you." Oh yes, I remember now how I felt next. How dare you say that to me? But I did not voice it. I kept it safe inside me. In fact, I have kept it safe inside me up until now! It must be the wine. I feel kind of warm and glowing inside, as if courage finds me willing to confront this most dramatic of moments in my life.

How do you actually deal with the fact that, by the age of 12, you have had three stepfathers, when your real father is finally revealed? It is not easy. There is no background knowledge of how to deal with this sort of thing. All sorts of thoughts go racing through your mind. Will I be able to meet him? Will I be able to have a father of my own after all?

The next question I finally summoned up to ask my mother was, "Who is my real father then?" Long, pregnant pause.

"Well, your real father is a Christian priest, actually a very special one. He was decorated during the war and was given the Knight of the Order of Orange Nassau with Swords (Dutch) 1946." This became my **first step towards learning about FORGIVENESS after the lies and deceit.**

My mother told me for a long time after the above revelation, that I had begged her to find my real father so I could meet him. That is absolutely not the truth. I never wanted to go searching for him. I wanted him to come searching for me! But my mother had other ideas. She yearned to get back to England to live there again. So my so-called desperation to meet my real father became her excuse to move us back to England. As soon as my younger sister was ready to start school and my older sister had finished her high school, it seemed a perfect time to move. By now, I was 13 and in the middle of my schooling. I was really sad to leave all my friends behind and my lovely school that I adored.

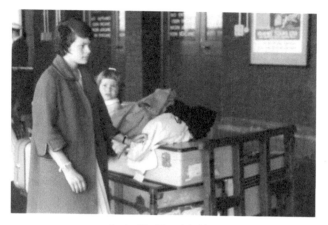

Arrival in Harwich 1961

CHAPTER 5

1961. A NEW LIFE BEGINS IN ENGLAND

We arrived in England with lots of money in the bank but no home. For months we stayed in a hotel by the seaside in Sussex, whilst my mother drove around South England to find us a perfect place to settle down. I would look after my adorable little sister whilst mother was gone.

By now, mother had found out where my real father was living, so she decided that we should live in Surrey (which was fairly close to where my father lived), where she bought a nice house for us to live in. I started attending a private school in Guildford. You can imagine how difficult it was for me to start schooling in a new country. My English was very limited, and it was agonizing trying to do my schoolwork. But somehow, I managed to settle in well and soon made some nice friends.

My mother seemed happy to finally be back home in the country she loved and where she had grown up. I was getting on quite well at school, much to everyone's surprise. In fact, I was often praised for my ability to adapt so easily, into a new language and school system.

I remember the first time my mother decided to take me to my real father's house. She would don her big sunglasses and head scarf as we set off. We would sit outside his house in our car, watching to see if he would either come out of his house or arrive home. Then she would ask me to go and ring his front doorbell and announce myself. When I objected, she would taunt me and tell me I was a coward and gutless. We would drive back home in stony silence. You see, I still had this notion that, if my father really loved me, he would come looking for me. It was not in my nature to go looking for him. Whenever my mother got angry with me, she used to tell me it would have been better if she'd had me adopted in the first place!

Shortly after we had moved into our new home, we started to attend the local church. A young and charismatic vicar had just joined our church, and my mother quickly formed a friendship with him. I started my confirmation classes with him and was confirmed one foggy night in a little church in the valley of the Surrey Downs. It was a complete out-of-body experience for me, and I saw many 'other beings' around me when I was being confirmed. To this day, I can still conjure up the events of that evening. The candles in the church, the holy atmosphere, the feeling of completeness.

1962. LIFE BEGINS WITH MY CRUEL UNCLE

Shortly after my confirmation, a drastic event happened in my life. My mother had a cousin, whom she had been very fond of since she was a young girl. For me, he was called Uncle John. He had a very powerful personality. 'Larger than life' was an expression often used for him. He was a very successful businessman, who had made a lot of money in the food and wine business. He had recently got divorced and was living in a large mansion with his staff. Shortly after my fourteenth birthday, my mother announced that I was going to spend some time with him in his home. He was, in fact, to become my guardian. I think this was a perfect solution for my mother, as I was still showing no signs of wanting to meet my real father. My mother must have felt I needed a fatherly influence.

The very first weekend I was to spend with my uncle, I was picked up by his chauffeur and driven to his posh London office. Later, we went to a famous restaurant, where we were joined by my uncle's son. The music was playing, and I had my first dance with my cousin on the dance floor. Around 9pm, my uncle and I left the restaurant. He drove us back to his house in his shiny Rolls Royce. We arrived there around 10pm, but there was no sign of his staff. My uncle showed me a beautiful bedroom that had been allocated to me as my very own. I was enthralled with the splendour of the furniture. When I opened the cupboard doors, it was full of designer clothes just for me. My uncle asked me to come and kiss him goodnight when I was ready for bed. Being young and innocent, I thought nothing of it and did as I was asked.

As I entered his bedroom, he was sitting at the edge of his bed in his pyjamas. I remember the television being on. I stood at a distance and shyly said, "Goodnight, Uncle."

He patted the space beside him on the bed and said, "Come and sit next to me and have a glass of hot milk." He poured a glass from a flask that had been placed on his bedside table by his staff. I went to sit on his bed when suddenly he pulled me onto it with a heavy force. It totally took me by surprise, and the next thing I knew, he was raping me. I do not know how to put this delicately, but you can imagine the worst.

After the ordeal, I remember rushing to my bedroom, flinging myself on the floor by my bed, sobbing, calling God's name, repeatedly asking, "Why, why me? What have I done to deserve this? Now no one will ever want to marry me." Then I heard a Voice responding, "Dearest girl, do not cry. I am here and will make sure that you come to no harm. I am in you, below you, around you and in front of you." How strange that Voice sounded. It felt so real. Could I be sure that I would be all right? I did feel very protected in that moment and chose to hold onto the truth of the words I had heard. I have since learnt that this was the Voice of my Guru, who would reveal Himself to me many years later. **My second step towards learning about FORGIVENESS.**

If you are not afraid of the Voice inside you, you will not be afraid of *the* Voice.

The next morning, I went down for breakfast but was told by the dining room staff that my uncle would not be joining me for breakfast. Did I eat anything? I honestly can't remember. Shortly afterwards, my uncle's son stopped by and asked me if I wanted to go to the shops to buy the latest Mash Potato record. We sped off in his sports car and came back laden with the latest pop records. Several hours were spent in the inner sitting room, with my cousin teaching me to dance the Mash Potato. It was like being in another world of normality, with the trauma of the night before being anaesthetised by the music and dancing.

When my uncle finally did make an appearance, he acted as if nothing had happened between us. Thoughts went through my mind that maybe I'd had a bad dream. Sadly, that was not the case. That night, it happened again, and so it went on. The usual threats of, "You must not tell anyone, it is our secret, no one will believe you" were issued. For any person who has not had a similar traumatic experience, it is difficult to explain how one is frozen and unable to escape, especially at such a young age.

My schoolwork suffered. Then it was decided that I was to be sent to boarding school. This was an imposing place, being Battle Abbey, the Castle built in 1066. Every other weekend, we were allowed exeats for the day. I would stand by the window in my dormitory, which looked out onto the long driveway towards the

Driveway at Battle Abbey, 1963

entrance gate, hoping against hope that my uncle would not appear. But soon I would see either his Rolls Royce or his E-Type Jaguar come driving up the driveway to take me out. Then the same thing would happen in his hotel room. Looking back, I am amazed how well I coped. I think I was just good at blocking these incidents out, as most of my memories are of various places we would travel to.

Holidays were spent with my mother or my uncle, who would take me sailing on his yacht, which was moored in Cannes, south of France. Usually, some important people would join us on our cruises around the Mediterranean.

Often, my uncle would drive us to Brighton, staying at the Metropolitan hotel, where there was a posh casino. My uncle was well known there, as he was a great gambler. At the age of 15 and 16, he took me into the casino, where he would then win tons of money and name me his lucky mascot!

He would also take me to the Savoy Hotel Restaurant, where he had his own table right opposite Noel Coward's table, who, more often than not, would be sitting there on his own. I remember him spending a lot of time looking over at our table.

My time with my mother was beginning to suffer. She treated me like a maid when I was in her house and was often verbally abusive. She was giving out the message that I was not good enough and I did not matter, although deep down I knew that she did love me. It took every ounce of my self-worth to hold onto who I was, knowing I was not a bad person, just up against some strange adults that were not being supportive in my adolescent years. Looking back, it seems that my mother was slipping into a deep depression. I have come to the conclusion that, at some level, my mother must have known what was happening to me at the hands of my uncle, but she chose to ignore it.

I have now come to understand that the most authentic thing about us as humans is our capacity to endure, to overcome, to transform, to love and to be greater than our suffering. **At this point, I was on my way to the third step towards learning about FORGIVENESS at a deeper level**.

Me age 15

CHAPTER 6

1962. I TURN TO GOD FOR HELP

It was during this time, that I first started to turn to God in earnest. I loved going to our Sunday church services during school term, as I was now boarding. We also had a lovely little chapel inside the school, where we could go to by ourselves to pray. Most nights I would be in there for ages having chats with God. One night during my prayers, I was shown in a vision that I had "walked with Jesus" during His time of preaching. I had been one of His followers and loved him dearly: I still do to this day.

God became my dearest friend. Whenever I was particularly upset about something, I would pop into the little chapel and have a chat with my very best friend. I felt that God always listened to me. It was during this time that a strange thing happened. I asked God why I had to endure the repeated abuse from my uncle, when I became aware of that VOICE again saying that it was something I *had* to go through and to be brave and trusting. Many times since, I have speculated on whether I had to go through it because I had been an abuser myself in a past life. What goes around comes around? **The fourth step towards FORGIVENESS.**

Years later in India, I had a Nadi reading, when it became evident why I'd had to experience all the traumas life had offered me. Amongst other things, I was told that in a past life, I had not been a good child to my parents, or siblings, or a good spouse, so in this life, after having asked for liberation, I had to relive the experience of how it felt like to be an abuser on many levels. Karma had to be burnt up. I remember after having this reading, I felt a big 'aha' moment, when suddenly things started to make sense, and I understood why I had to experience things that were out of my control. It no longer became a question of

WHY ME? You have to be very strong when your soul calls forth for Liberation! Many times I have heard Sai devotees ask Sai Baba for Liberation and He has responded, "Are you sure?", indicating that if you want Liberation, a lot of karma has to be burnt off and it can be a very difficult and painful journey.

Nadi Astrology is an ancient super science that sheds light on the journey of your soul and helps you understand your past, present and future. Also known as Nadi Jyotish, Nadi is the Science of Thumbprints and the Science of Sounds. The great sages of India have etched some peoples' destinies on palm leaves as divine predictions. Their sight into the future has shown them the difficulties that would prevail in modern times for these people. Out of their deep compassion for humanity, these advanced and accelerated beings wanted to provide an opportunity for people to discover and transform their destinies and evolve their souls. The soul stories that they saw were written down. This mystical science from our ancient Seers not only gives predictions but also remedies to dissolve your karma and course correct your life in the right direction.

In ancient times, information was passed down orally. The written word came 3000 years after that. That was when scribes started to record much of India's literary, scientific, spiritual and astrological heritage of over a thousand of years. Granite slabs, thin copper plates and tree bark were some of the mediums used for recording information, but for the Nadi information, leaves of palm were the choice.

The Rishis had special scribes carefully etch each letter of a person's story into the dried leaf with a special tool or stylus. This was all done by hand, to avoid splitting the leaf. The writing was almost always continuous, without any space between words. This is one reason why the reading of the leaves requires training, as well as an understanding of the ancient languages of Tamil or Sanskrit. When the etching was complete, lamp-black or turmeric was applied to increase the contrast and make it readable, then oil was rubbed in to help preserve them. A bundle of leaves in the same thumbprint category, or soul grouping, were then bound with a cord between two wooden covers.

It seems as if we are a collection of our karma. When we start burning them up, our Soul is making progress.

When I was 16, the Christmas holidays saw my uncle and I travel to Cape Town in South Africa. He had broken his foot, which was in a cast, and I was supposed to look after him. He had a lot of his business in the food industry in South Africa, such as exotic tinned food and a famous brand of Sherry. We stayed at the Mount Nelson hotel, where I mostly spent my time at the pool reading. By now, I was getting quite good at avoiding my uncle when it came to bedtime. After dinner, I would get talking to people in the hotel, then sneak off to my bedroom without him seeing that I had gone. When later I heard knocking on my door, I would not open it, pretending I was asleep. In the morning, I would rise early and have a lovely breakfast on the open terrace.

One evening, I was invited by one of my uncle's clients to go out for dinner with their teenage children. Finding no excuse to refuse this without it looking strange, my uncle had to accept the invitation on my behalf. I was super excited to go on a sort of date with these rich young people. We went to the most expensive restaurant in Cape Town, and I ordered a steak to eat. When it arrived, I must have been so nervous that when I started cutting into it, it somehow flew off my plate and landed in my lap. I was so embarrassed, I did not know where to look. But everyone thought it terribly funny, and the rest of the evening went by without any further embarrassing events. When I was deposited back at the hotel, I ran to my room, passing my uncle's room, seeing one shoe outside the door to be polished, so I knew he had already retired for the night.

Me age 17

CHAPTER 7

1965. MY LAST DAYS AT SCHOOL

July 1965 saw my last term at school. I had passed all my drama and elocution exams. I was thrilled when I was chosen to join the National Youth Theatre during the summer holidays. That was the year when Timothy Dalton, Helen Mirren and Timothy West were there as well. I had a wonderful month training and I fell in love with the theatre.

The following month, for the last time, I went sailing on my uncle's yacht with him. We flew to France and picked up the yacht in Cannes, where it was moored and where my eldest sister was waiting to join us. One afternoon, we arrived in the port of Naples and asked my uncle if we could go shopping. As we walked the streets of Naples, we realised that we were being followed by two young men, each in their own open-top red sports cars. We finally stopped, and as we did, they stopped as well. They sprang out of their cars and came over to introduce themselves. We daringly agreed to have a coffee with them in a little café. They were so charming these two Italian brothers, as they turned out to be. It was refreshing being with them, instead of the constant stuffy company of my uncle. What a fun time we had, laughing, joking and enjoying ourselves.

We accepted their invitation to meet them after dinner, when they would show us the sights of Naples and take us to a nightclub up in the hills. After dinner, my sister and I told my uncle what we were going to do, and he got seriously angry. But we ran down the gangplank anyway and found our two handsome Italians waiting for us by their sportscars. We drove in the barmy night air up the hill, arriving at the nightclub, which had spectacular views over Naples. For a few hours, I was in heaven, dancing for the first time with a person close to my own age, and it felt wonderful. I wanted the night to go on forever, but they were gentlemen, deciding they'd better take us back to the yacht before we got into even more trouble.

We arrived back at the yacht, where my uncle was standing at the top of the gangplank. He was drunk, and I could smell the fumes from several feet away. He was dangling a gold bracelet in his hand and weaving from side to side, saying, "You see, I was going to give you this tomorrow as an early Christmas present, but I have decided to feed it to the fish instead." With that, he dropped it into the sea.

As he did this, I scooted past him, narrowly missing being clouted across the head, and said, "See if I care."

From then on, it was war between my uncle and myself. I did not confess to my sister what had been happening to me over the past couple of years.

One interesting observation about my eldest sister: For some reason, my mother had put my sister's father's name down on my birth certificate, instead of my real father's name. My mother felt this was only right, as she was still married to her first husband, my eldest sister's father, when I was born. But my sister made it very clear to me that when her father passed away, I was not to claim from his estate. In Denmark, every child who bears a man's name on their birth certificate automatically inherits in equal share with any other sibling of the same father! Being the good girl I am, of course I did not pursue it.

Another interesting observation is, that my grandmother from my mother's side also said to me that I would not inherit anything from her when the time came. She wanted to give to my older sister, as her father had been so good to her. My sister was always very spoilt by her father, who was very rich. When I was younger and we lived in Denmark, she would sometimes take me with her when she visited him at weekends. He was such fun to be with and gave us many wonderful times. He once told me he wished I had been his daughter, as I was always such a help. When my sister was 21, he gave her a beautiful cottage in the countryside, where we spent many happy times. I don't remember ever being jealous of my sister, I just felt mostly like an outsider, not worthy of much.

On our return from our trip around the Mediterranean on my uncle's yacht, it was decided I would take a secretarial course. I hated it. I was still living in my uncle's house but avoided him as much as possible. I had managed to tell him, just after I turned 16 years of age, that I was not prepared to tolerate his abuse and if he persisted, I would have no option but to tell someone. So it stopped. But he became an even heavier drinker.

One day, when I returned home from my

secretarial school, I found him drunk at the top of the stairs, shouting at me. As I passed him on the stairs, he went to hit me, but as I ducked, he lost his balance, stumbling down the stairs, and broke his foot again. My uncle went into hospital with all sorts of complications from his broken foot, war wounds and diabetes.

After visiting him at the Harley Street Clinic, where he was hospitalized, I had a car accident as I was crossing Oxford Circus, which had a wooden ramp over it, as there was some construction work being carried out underground. My car ended upside down in a shop window. Within seconds, dozens of fire trucks arrived. I was unhurt but very shaken.

I called my uncle's butler and asked him to come and pick me up from the train station by my uncle's house. When I got off the train and into his car, I could smell alcohol coming from him. We drove past my uncle's house. He turned into the little lane by the house, stopped the car and proceeded to attack me. I managed to escape and ran back to the house, locking myself into my room.

A few days later, when a girlfriend asked me if I would share a flat with her in London, I made my escape and never went back again to the drama of life in my uncle's house. Isn't it strange that no one suspected what I had to endure for those past years?

I was turning into a not too bad looking young lady with impeccable manners. My dress sense was immaculate, as I loved putting outfits on with everything matching.

Even though I had very little money, what a relief those carefree days in London were. I started to have a feeling that I wanted to study to become a psychiatrist but had no means of supporting myself while studying. Instead, I signed up at a modelling school, majoring as student No.1, and shortly after was inundated with modelling work. Only now do I realise that I could have easily asked my uncle to support me back then. But the thought never crossed my mind.

My marriage to Piers age 19

CHAPTER 8

1967. MY MARRIAGE TO PIERS

About 6 months later, being 19 years old, I met a nice gentleman, who was a director of a big fashion company. We got married a few months later. It was decided by my mother that my uncle was to give me away. What a nightmare that was for me. Although he had accepted that he could no longer abuse me, he was still very fond of me, pretending to the world, as he had done all along, what a wonderful substitute father he was to me!

After my mother and little sister left for the church, my uncle said it would be nice to have a drink. All I could find in the house was an open bottle of port. Demolishing the bottle, he became a bit tipsy. Having had a glass myself to calm my nerves, I felt very flushed in my cheeks. We arrived at the church, and I had to support my uncle up the aisle, as my husband-to-be stood waiting for me. I kept reminding myself that soon I would be free from the bondage of my uncle to start my new life, married to a sweet, gentleman.

I had to pay for my own wedding with some of the money in a Trust Fund my adopted father had left me, as well as the engagement party my mother decided to hold for herself that same evening, after my husband and I had departed for our honeymoon. This was now her fourth marriage she was embarking on, and I expect she had announced it to upstage me at my own wedding. She had in fact suggested we have a double wedding on the same day, but I told her firmly that was not an option.

What a disaster our supposed honeymoon was. As my husband had just started a new job as director for a big fashion company in Coventry, he decided we had to drive all the way up to Oxfordshire to our new home we had bought to celebrate it there. When we arrived at the house, he had mislaid the front door key. Eventually, we got in by breaking a window. I was exhausted and had seriously lost my sense of humour by that time. It was not a good start to our marriage, especially as he left early for work the next day.

Married life started in quaint old Cromwell Cottage on top of Edgehill, which my small trust fund had allowed us to buy. I was very isolated in this beautiful but strange place, hardly seeing my husband except for on the weekends, when he was mostly exhausted. I spent my time teaching myself to cook and went for many solitary walks in the countryside. I would often feel as if I had spent time there in the distant past, as I must have been a soldier fighting during the Battle of Edgehill with Oliver Cromwell! It was the same feeling I'd had when I'd gone to boarding school at Battle Abbey. I often felt as if I had been there fighting during the time of the Battle of Hastings.

It was while I lived at Cromwell Cottage that I found out my mother had forged my signature to gain access to some money my adopted father had left me, after he had cashed in his Insurance Policy, just before he had committed suicide. She had plenty of her own, as he'd left her a fortune, so why she had to do that, God only knows. I was a bit upset to think that my own mother could do such a thing to her daughter. **Another opportunity for forgiveness.**

Nine months after our marriage, my husband was transferred to New York City. So there I was, just turned 20, dumped in the hotel room, as my husband left for work the following morning of our arrival. I was simply terrified. Those were the days when it was not safe to walk the streets of that crime-ridden city. Somehow, I managed to pull myself together and soon got friendly with this amazing city. I found us a beautiful apartment on East End Avenue, opposite Gracie Mansion.

Once we were settled into our new home, I started to look for work. Within days, I landed myself a job with an advertising agent. I was 20 and in my prime. Everyone loved my English accent, and I made many friends there.

During this time, I never saw my husband. He used to leave early in the morning and come home late at night. We drifted apart very quickly. It became evident that we did not have a marriage as such, therefore the inevitable happened and we separated. I was now on my own in New York at the age of 21. I am happy to say though that my ex-husband and I remained friends throughout his life. It felt good when he confessed some years later that he wasn't really cut out for marriage, as he was a workaholic, therefore I was not to feel bad about the unsuccess of it.

CHAPTER 9

1969. FILMING IN NEW YORK

Sometime later, after branching out on my own, having stayed in the Lady's Barbican Hotel for a while, I met a film director, whom I started dating. Shortly after, I moved in with him. He had three children, who used to stay with us every other weekend. They were great kids and I adored them. My new boyfriend and I worked hard and made many commercials and short films together.

Once, when we were filming in San Francisco, one evening after dinner, the crew were sitting smoking a joint. I had never experienced drugs before but was encouraged to take a puff. Just one puff was enough for me to have a violent reaction. I started having hallucinations and it was only due to my boyfriend staying close to me for 24 hours, making sure I did not fall into a coma, that I came out of it. I swore never to touch drugs again. One of the hallucinations I had during those 24 hours was of an old man's head stuck on a pole with blood pouring from it.

My boyfriend and I talked about having children ourselves, but I was not keen on the idea until my divorce came through. As my estranged husband wanted us to have an uncontested divorce, I would have to wait three years before it could become final.

But it wasn't long before I started getting very broody, and there was talk about us having a baby before my divorce came through. Just as I got pregnant, we signed a deal with Lee Remick to make a film in Spain. Suddenly, my boyfriend announced it was NOT OK for me to be pregnant after all. The word 'inconvenient' was branded about. We separated after a big fight, when he told me to terminate the pregnancy.

This was truly the hardest thing I ever had to do. Worse than the nightmare about who my real father was, worse than my uncle's unacceptable behaviour, worse than my mother's strange behaviour. I can still feel the sadness of that day, feeling desolate and lonely as I entered the clinic. Knowing I would never be able to forgive myself, yet knowing at the same time that I was not capable of bringing up a child by myself, I felt I had no other choice. The issue of termination is so huge. To touch upon it opens a large wound that never seems to want to heal. The guilt and despair are very evident in a poem I found about this sad event:

Shall I not feel it deeply now it has gone?
Shall I not think of it at night, its light my light?
Will there not be pain inside me,
That life unlived but loved, is ended thus?

This is then the time, this is the test,
Nor is it given to me to know which was best
For this short time it has lived.
In this short hour it has died.

For this is the moment as undefined
Of child unknown, unborn
The bitter wind of death has blown.

As my Spiritual Teacher had said to me, "Sometimes a little mad!" This must have been the maddest thing I have ever done. Will I ever forgive myself? Will I ever be forgiven?

Sometimes you get so desperate that you have no option but to start taking control of your life and transforming it into something worthwhile. You start to clean out all the corners of your mind that have been occupying you to the point of despair. This then opens up a space to grow. After a while, this became a turning point in my life, when the suffering became more bearable. I had no option but to fall in love with something much bigger than myself or the world I had created around me. **The fifth step towards FORGIVENESS.**

Roman Polanski 1970

CHAPTER 10

1970. MY TIME WITH ROMAN POLANSKI

I went back to live in England in 1970 but still felt very low. I was lucky enough to be able to rent a room in a girlfriend's flat in London, where I could try to piece my life back together. Vaguely, I heard the phone ring one day. When I answered it, another friend of mine told me that a famous film director was searching for someone to look after his personal affairs whilst starting a new film. I was not told who the director was. Instinct kicked in and I decided to turn up for the appointment. The following day, I arrived at an office in Park Lane for my interview. A few minutes later, a charismatic man walked into the waiting room. There was an instant ancient recognition between us. It was none other than Roman Polanski. We talked for a while, and without further ado, he asked me to start working for him the next day.

A year before I met Roman, his wife, Sharon Tate, had been murdered by Susan Denise Atkins, who was a member of the Charles Manson gang family, on 9 August 1969 in their rented house 10050 Cielo Drive, Benedict Canyon, Los Angeles. Roman and Sharon had been expecting their first baby. She was 8 months pregnant. It was later discovered that Charles Manson was in a revenge mood to take down Doris Day's son, whom he'd had a falling out with over a song demo he had submitted, which had been rejected. It was Sharon and some friends who were, on that fateful day, living in Doris Day's son's house while Roman was in London trying desperately to finish the script for "The Day of The Dolphin" so he could join his wife before she gave birth.

When I started working for Roman, almost a year after this huge tragedy, he was still very fragile. His friends were very worried for his mental state, as his obsession about finding his wife's killer had taken a toll on him. First, he had to go through the panic and disbelief that he would never see his beloved wife again. He could not grasp the thin moment that separated her existence from nothingness. After that came a period of utter grief that lasted as long as the investigation. Those two were parallel until the obsession of the crime was solved. Then came the dismissal and withdrawal from the event. As Roman was no stranger to tragic events from his childhood, from his brush with death in the ghetto when he was attacked by a murderer, as well as the final knowledge that his mother had been gassed in a concentration camp, he had probably summoned a superhuman courage to deal with horrific events.

Roman was also suffering from the outrageous press that he and the murder of his wife were generating. In his own words, the reporting about Sharon and the murders was virtually criminal. The press were blaming the victims for their own murders! They put in everything they could imagine. Roman says that the victims were assassinated two times, once by the murderers, the second time by the press. In fact, he goes as far as to say that the press who write "personal" accounts of what they claim to know make a lot of money off the case. One wonders if the people who wrote those articles are any better than the murderers.

What makes the press so vituperative?

After the murder of his wife, everything he considered to film seemed futile. He could not think of a subject that was worthwhile or dignified enough to spend a year or more on, in view of what had happened to him. In the state of his mind, it seemed more acceptable to settle on filming Macbeth, as he loved Shakespeare, and it was worth the effort.

It is hard to look back on that time, when, at the age of 22, I had this huge responsibility to become his PA. But Roman had seen something in me that he identified with and called me his Angel.

Here we were, two souls, who had both lost a child each, although under different circumstances. Hence, we had a deep understanding and connection with each other.

One day, after the new company Rolls Royce had been delivered to our office in Park Lane, he asked me if I would accompany him to the theatre to see a production of "The Mouse Trap". I accepted with great joy, and off we drove, sitting in the back of the Rolls, on our way to the theatre. But all was not well. The car started to cough and splutter down Park Lane. Soon, fumes were coming into the car, making us feel sick. Our chauffeur jumped out of the car. We had to abandon it there and then, taking a taxi to the theatre instead. Halfway through watching "The Mouse Trap", we looked at each other, having the same thought: "This is boring, shall we escape?" As soon as it was intermission, we ran out the door of the theatre like two naughty school children and ended up having a quick bite to eat, then went back to his house in Eaton Place Mews. We had a lovely way of being together, a gentle energy between us, but we also made each other laugh, which was lovely to witness, as Roman was still suffering from the loss of his great love, Sharon.

Another incident I remember was when we went to the famous Tramp nightclub in London. I had bought a beautiful Ossie Clark outfit and apparently looked pretty amazing in it. Roman and I had a few dances, but mostly he was talking to friends, one of whom was Robert Evans. Robert had recently married Ali MacGraw, and both he and Roman were commenting on how much I looked like her. Robert kept asking me to dance, but I had no interest except for being near Roman. Later that evening came the set up! Roman asked Robert to take me home in a taxi. When we arrived outside my apartment, he tried to invite himself in. I would have none of it, so predictably it was not exactly well received. The next morning, I asked Roman what the big idea was. He smiled and said, "Just testing."

It was soon time to go on location in Llandudno, North Wales, where we had taken over the Port Marion Hotel for the entire cast and crew, as well as ourselves. Roman had insisted I should stay in Angel Cottage, with his cottage only a few doors away. As Roman went ahead of me, I arrived a few days later, traveling up on the train with a big group of VIP guests.

On the train journey, someone produced a brownie cake, which was my big misfortune to eat, as without realizing it, I had consumed a rather large quantity of hashish. I was not used to taking recreational drugs so had a strong reaction, a bit like the one I'd had when I was filming in San Francisco. By the time we arrived in Llandudno, I was slightly out of my head and kept saying, "Where is Roman?" I must confess, I was secretly a bit in love with him, on a level which is difficult to explain. When we arrived in Port Merrion, well after midnight, someone must have gone to Roman's cottage and told him I was not in the best of health.

The next thing I knew, there was a loud knock on my door and a familiar voice saying, "Leonora, open up, it's me." I managed to stagger to the door and saw my sweet Roman standing there looking very worried. He put his arms around me and said, "I know, fresh air is what you need." Without even thinking of himself, he took off his beautiful warm coat (it was early winter when we were there), helped me put it on, then guiding me outside. Up and down the road we walked until I felt a bit more normal. He then took me to my cottage, tucked me into bed and said, "Sleep well, little angel. See you in the morning."

Many hours later, I woke up and found he had left his coat for me to use when I got up. Strangely, I felt ok and was just longing to be united with Roman again to thank him for his gentle kindness. Later that day, he asked his chauffeur to take me into town to get me some warmer clothes. Such thoughtfulness from him always touched me.

Filming started in earnest on Macbeth. The weather was filthy, and after a long day in the cold, we all used to gather in the big dining hall and eat together. Roman would often ask me to sit next to him, and I always loved being in his company. Eventually, the inevitable happened and we started a relationship, which was gentle, but at the same time unrealistic. We both knew that Roman was too damaged at this time to commit to anything but comfort from a little angel. I was also too young and not in tune with the way of life of high-powered VIP film people. But the time we spent together was very special. At night, Roman would tell me about his extraordinary childhood, when he had been separated from his parents at the beginning of the war, his mother having been taken to a concentration camp and his father nowhere to be found. He'd had to look after himself from the age of 8 in and around the Krakow ghetto. Although he was looked after by different families during this time, therefore usually had a place to sleep at night, during the day, he was mostly left to his own devises, to roam about as he pleased. Sometimes, he would wake up at night having had a flashback from those ghastly times, which no child should have had to endure.

The time came when I knew I had to leave before I got too hurt. My last day in Llandudno was sad. The chauffeur was to pick me up after lunch and take me to the train station on my way to reuniting with my own special journey that lay ahead for me. We were sitting in the big dining room, and Roman and I were sitting next to each other. There were only moments left. Suddenly, he took my hand and said, "Come." We went to the end of the dining room into a quiet corner and hugged and hugged. Then he whispered in my ear, "Make sure you find a good man, Leonora. I am sorry I cannot be the one, but when you do find him, I want to meet him and make sure he is good enough for you." I was very moved by his concern for me, as had always been the case. My heart was heavy, wondering how I was to tell it that my time with this extraordinary man was over. The dream is to have a true connection with another human being, and I had experienced that.

We stayed in touch by letter from time to time and met again when I introduced him to what I believed was 'the good man'.

95 WEST EATON PLACE MEWS
LONDON · SW1

Mrs Leonora Vawn,
26 The Links,
21 Sutherland Street,
Nutral Bay,
2089 N.S.W. Australia.   1st July 1974.

Dear Leonora,

Going through a file of accumulated mail I just found your
letter. As you know, I am not the Fastest Pen in the West,
and then I received your letter in the midst of work on
CHINATOWN.

I hope you are still well and successful and I'm sorry you
are not now around - obviously your trip to Europe you
were threatening us with didn't come off yet.

Love and kisses,

Roman

Roman Polanski

P.S. Thank you for the clipping and the Allen Jones table
story thrilled me to death - beware of Women's Lib!

(Dictated by Mr Polanski but signed in his absence)

Letter from Roman Polanski

THE FRENCH PHOTOGRAPHER
AND CHARLES AZNAVOUR

When I got back to London, I travelled for a while with a French photographer friend of mine, who was working on a film with Charles Aznavour. What a charming man Charles was, but he did not speak a word of English. I urged him to learn the language so he could sing his famous songs in English. This he did. Soon, his songs were translated, and I felt honoured to have been a small part of that.

Canberra 1971

CHAPTER 11

1972. OFF TO AUSTRALIA

Shortly after my time with Roman, I got glandular fever. I was quite unwell for months, unable to leave my room. I had rented a lovely room in Knightsbridge, in a private house. My landlady's ex-husband was a GP, so I was beautifully looked after by both of them. When I started to get better, the GP suggested I take a cruise for a complete cure. A girlfriend of mine was just about to set sail for Australia, so the next thing I knew, I was sailing on the P&O 'Canberra' cruise ship to 'Down Under'. As we entered Perth, a film crew came aboard to

Me and Girlfriend on board Canberra

film part of a documentary they were doing for P&O. It was generally known on board that I was an actress and model. Before I knew it, I was signed up to do some filming for the documentary. By the time we arrived in Sydney, I had been given the name of a top acting/model agency and was soon signed up on their books.

My girlfriend and I quickly found a beautiful little flat in Rose Bay, overlooking the water, right opposite the famous Doyle's restaurant. Work was plentiful. Most days I would be filming commercials or short parts in TV shows. The film director, who had 'discovered' me on board the P&O ship, started calling me, asking me out for dates. He was such a nice man. We had wonderful times together. This was the best time to be in Sydney, a young and upcoming city, with heavenly places to live and beaches to die for. It was a good tonic for me to live in the glorious sunshine and sea air. My health returned to normal, and I was thriving.

Mostly, I was busy working to pay for rent and food. Life was good. I was soon known as the "Colgate Girl" as almost every day I would be seen on the TV, flashing my perfect teeth in the Colgate commercial. I had also made a commercial with Paul Hogan, who was fun to talk to. It was a huge privilege to get the lead part in a documentary film called *She's a Lady* for P&O. We set sail around the South Pacific, visiting many exotic places like Tonga, Fiji, Thailand and Indonesia. It was a truly memorable experience, and the cast and crew were terrific.

Left: filming "Luke's Kingdom" and Above: filming "She is a Lady"

But the funniest moment in filming was on *Luke's Kingdom* with Oliver Tobias. In one scene, which was being filmed in a wood, we had to sit in a horse and cart to go off on a romantic drive. Suddenly, the horse bolted and we went racing down the woody lane, wondering what would happen next. We clung to each other in terror, but finally the horse tired and came to a standstill. After the initial fright, we could not stop laughing until we were finally rescued by the film crew. From then on, a sweet friendship developed, until Oliver had to leave Sydney after the filming ended.

MY TIME WITH TERRY

This was when the feeling started again about wanting to start a family. By now, I was 26. I had been going out with my lovely film director for two years. He was not interested in getting married or having children, as he had already been married and had two wonderful boys, whom I adored. I got on very well with his ex-wife, so all was going smoothly. Still, the nagging feeling of wanting to get married and having children of my own persisted. Finally, I decided that I had to cut my ties with my lovely boyfriend to give myself a chance to meet someone who did want to get married and have children.

CHAPTER 12

1974. I MEET THE DUTCHMAN

It was a few months after the sad parting with Terry that I met a man who was on a business trip to Sydney. He had been invited to a barbeque by friends, where I was also a guest for the weekend. In walked this very handsome Dutch man. Our eyes met and that was it. It was like another very ancient feeling, that we knew each other from a previous life. Within 24 hours, he had proposed to me. I accepted!

After the weekend and feeling as if I was floating on a cloud, I opened the door to my apartment and heard the phone ring. I rushed breathlessly to answer it, and as I did, heard a very dear familiar voice. "Where have you been? I have been trying to get you all weekend." My old boyfriend was almost shouting in desperation down the phone (no mobile phones in those days). I told him I had been away for a couple of days staying with friends. He said we must meet NOW and asked if he could come round. He sounded so desperate, I said, "Of course."

I opened the front door, and there stood my dear love of the past few years. He looked as if he had not slept for days. He flung his arms around me, hugging me as if he would never let go. After disentangling myself and leading him to a chair, I asked what was the matter.

He looked at me and said with such love and tenderness, "Darling, I cannot live without you. I want to marry you and have children with you. Please say you will marry me."

I just sat there staring at him, not saying a word. Hundreds of thoughts were racing through my mind: Dear God, why so late? I have met another man who feels right. What should I do? PLEASE HELP ME! Then I told him the whole story of the weekend party and meeting this Dutch man, who had stolen my heart, which was unoccupied at the time. We had a deep connection, had so many things in common, that we had decided to leave as soon as possible for Europe to get married. I thought my old boyfriend would shout at me, but now it was his turn to be stunned into silence. Naturally, his first words were, "But how could you fall in love with someone so soon?"

Yes, well, how do we? I could not answer; I just sat staring at the floor, inwardly screaming, Oh God,

PLEASE HELP ME!

The silence seemed to last forever. I think we both started to cry. It was a sad, tender moment. I felt so powerless, as if the world had landed me the most humongous problem, which I did not know how to deal with. After a while, a very valid question was asked.

"So where is this Dutch man now?"

I explained, "He has gone to New Zealand on a business trip for a few days, then he is coming back to Sydney, when we will be leaving for Bali for a few days before returning to Rome."

My old boyfriend replied, "Do you know which hotel he is staying in?"

"No," I answered.

It was strange that I was so confident. Even though I did not know where this Dutchman was staying, I knew he would come back for me. Yes, I know, totally crazy! My old boyfriend was determined to find this new love of mine, so he proceeded to call several five-star hotels in New Zealand. After the third try, he got an operator saying, yes, there was a man by that name registered in the hotel, but he was out. He left a message for him to call back as soon as he got in.

A very long and heart-wrenching few hours went by. We cried a lot, but I was determined that I had to leave with this new man. It was as if all those months, when I had made it clear that I wanted to marry my old love and he had said no, I had hardened myself against him, now no longer able to let him enter the recess of my heart, where the dream of having children won over.

Then the phone rang. I answered it and felt my heart skip a beat to hear his voice. Tender words were spoken, then I had to tell him that my old boyfriend was sitting next to me and wanted to speak to him. I handed the phone to Terry, and he very politely asked, "Are you serious about taking Leonora back to Europe to marry her? Because if you are not, I want to know now, as I want to marry her myself." The answer was, yes, he was quite sure that he was coming back for me and we were getting married, if that was still my wish.

So that was that. Terry and I sat for a while longer, did some more crying, then said goodbye. But Terry did not leave it at that. When he got back home, he called his ex-wife, who had become a very dear girlfriend of mine. She then called me and started to shout down the phone at me, which was very uncharacteristic of her, being a mild-mannered lady. She was actually very concerned for me. She knew that I had just been selected to host a Current Affairs TV program and was up for a lead part in a film. In fact, I was one of Australia's most well-paid models/actresses at the time. She also insisted that Terry was absolutely certain he wanted to marry me. He had even told her I could have as many children as I liked! I said there was nothing to be done. I had made up my mind, I was leaving the following week.

The next week flew by, packing up my belongings and putting my furniture into storage, cancelling film and modelling contracts at great cost, saying goodbye to friends, seeing Terry for the last time (again many tears). I was still longing to see my new love again, excited about the prospect of our life together. Robert arrived duly in Sydney to pick me up. My old boyfriend and his ex-wife came to the airport to say goodbye to me and I suspect to suss out Robert. It was good to see him again, although there was a deep sadness leaving all my friends behind, plus my work and wonderful life. Still, that pull in my heart let me know that I was doing the right thing!

We arrived in Bali and had an idyllic week there. We had so many things in common and gently moved into a beautiful friendship. I was so happy! We called my mother in England, sitting together, telling her that we would shortly be back in Europe and she was to get ready for our wedding. She asked me a few questions like, 'Who is he?', 'Are you sure of who he is?', and the other usual questions a mother asks her daughter when she calls up to say she is about to marry a complete stranger. I told her not to worry, that he was gorgeous, married once, now divorced, and had a young son whom he loved very much. Most importantly, he wanted us to have children as soon as possible.

We left Bali a few days later, having spent some of the happiest times of my life. I felt that life simply could not get better. I felt I had arrived in paradise and that was where I wanted to stay. Our next stop was Hong Kong, where we were to stay for a few days for Robert to attend a business meeting. I remember us booking into a beautiful hotel, then doing a bit of shopping before having dinner. I thought Robert had been unusually quiet that day, as if there was something on his mind.

A couple of times, I would take his hand and say, "Darling, are you alright?" He would say yes, but it did not sound convincing.

That evening, he took my hand at the dinner table after a delicious meal and said, "Darling, I have something very important to tell you."

My heart stopped a beat. The last time someone had said that same sentence, it had been when my mother had informed me about my adopted father's suicide and my real father being alive. So I bravely said, "Yeeees?"

Robert said, "You know I told you I had one son? Well, actually, I have two." My face must have lit up, and I heard myself say, "Who cares how many children you have? I don't. But why did you say you only had one?"

Robert replied, "Well, I have not been completely honest with you ... I am still married."

My whole world stopped in that one moment. I felt paralysed. I felt like I wanted to die. I did not want to hear this. It was too much for me to cope with. So I just froze. We left the dining room, and for hours, I lay on my bed, staring at the ceiling. I can't remember actually thinking about anything in particular, just lying there. I do remember Robert kneeling at the bed, holding my hand, saying, "Darling, please say something, just as long as it's not that you want to leave me. I cannot live without you."

Many, many weary hours later, I finally managed to say I would not leave him. But I did not feel the same person any longer. I had no background knowledge of how to deal with something like this. My dream lay shattered at my feet. I would find it hard to live with this, especially having burnt all my bridges back in Australia, born on lies and deceit. **The sixth step towards FORGIVENESS.**

Somehow, I managed to scrape myself up from the floor and start all over again. It was not easy. Mostly, the next days were a blur. We arrived back in Rome, where we stayed in a rented apartment. Robert was very sweet and attentive, making sure while he was at work that I was looked after by his various friends, who would show me around Rome. I even managed to get a walk-on part in a film that Diana Ross was staring in.

Robert and I took his boys skiing in Switzerland over the Christmas holidays and met up with my friends, Roman Polanski and Gene Gutowski. They had invited us to come and spend some time with them, after I called informing them that I had met the 'good man'.

Our first night was spent having dinner as Roman's guests in a restaurant. There were about twelve of us sitting at a long table, including Gene Gutowski. I was content seeing Roman again, feeling he was in a happy, good place himself. (At the end of this chapter, you will be able to read the letter Gene Gutowski wrote to me about how concerned he was after introducing Robert to him.)

The following morning, we all met up on the ski slopes. I am not a very experienced skier, so what I thought I was doing when everyone said "Let's go to the top and race down" I do not know. But bravely, I took the ski lift up the mountain. We started to ski down the mountain as it began to snow heavily. I lost my way and took a wrong turn. I had a crash and hit my head on an ice block. I don't remember much, except I managed to walk for a while, eventually bumping into other skiers, who took me down the mountain. I was not feeling well and had a very bad headache.

The following day, we decided to fly back to Rome as my headache was getting quite serious. I was taken directly to a hospital, where a friend of ours, who was a neurosurgeon, looked after me. I was given a brain scan but got a violent reaction to the dye injected up my vein to the brain. Then I was put on strong antihistamines to counteract the reaction. I was in hospital for days.

Shortly after I got out of the hospital, I discovered I was pregnant. This was a planned pregnancy, as Robert wanted a child with me as soon as possible, as he had mentioned when we'd met in Sydney. That evening, when I told Robert the news, he was thrilled.

But the following day, he called me from his office and told me he wanted to go back to his wife! What was going wrong with the script now? My first reaction was that if he wanted to go back to his wife, I would not stand in his way. I told him to come and get his belongings in our flat. He came with his supposed estranged wife. I remember sitting having a cup of tea with them. She knew nothing about me being pregnant. I told her I was quite happy to give my blessings for them to get back together; hopefully, they would work things out and be happy. They left. I fell on my bed and cried. But quickly I had to dry my tears and think of what I would do now. **The seventh step towards FORGIVENESS.**

Hours later, the phone rang. It was Robert saying, "Darling, I have made a dreadful mistake; I want to be with you." By now, I had just about had enough. I told him absolutely no way, that I had already arranged to fly back to Australia and was leaving the next day. Robert was at the airport the following morning, pleading with me not to go. I declined.

CHAPTER 13

1974. BACK IN AUSTRALIA

What I thought I would do back in Australia I simply do not know. I just had to get away to think for a while. I was two months pregnant, but all I knew was that I was keeping this baby. I booked into a small hotel and phoned Terry. When I told him the predicament I was in, his reply came quickly, "Marry me." What a guy. No wonder I had fallen in love with him and still loved him dearly. But I could not do that to him. I was still in love with Robert and hoped that we could work things out. I desperately wanted my baby to have a legal father, which was foremost on my mind.

Every day I would get a call from Robert; also, many letters arrived, which I still have to this day. They are beautiful letters, telling me how much he loved me and that he was doing everything in his power to sort himself out. He was saying that maybe we should start a new life in Australia. He talked endlessly about our unborn baby. He was so sure it was a girl, and he wanted her to be called Natasha. I just wanted him to be happy, either with or without me.

As the weeks went by, I got dreadfully ill with sinus problems. I went for my 1st trimester scan when, to my dismay, I found out I had a large cyst on my right ovary. It was imperative I be operated on immediately as my baby was at risk. I called my mother, who agreed that I should fly back to England the next day. When I arrived in London, I called Robert and told him I was about to be operated on.

CHAPTER 14

1975. BACK TO ENGLAND

After my operation to have my right ovary removed with the large cyst on it, I woke up in my big room in the London Clinic, with flowers all around me. My mother was sitting by my bed. I did not ask if I had cancer, though feared this might be the case, but uttered, "Is my baby still with me and alive?" The answer was "Yes." What a relief. Then I felt the most excruciating pain in my tummy. I screamed but was told I could not have any pain killers as it would harm the baby. For 48 hours I had to endure this unbearable pain. On the third day it subsided slightly.

The drive back to my mother's house was equally horrendous. Every bump in the road was like a knife being driven into my abdomen. Robert came for a weekend visit. It was good to see him again. I was still in love with him but did not want to be with him while he was a married man. He told me that no matter what, he was determined we would spend the rest of our lives together. Still the letters from him poured through the letterbox at my mother's house; still I waited to see what would happen.

We decided it would be best for me to stay with my mother for a while. Robert said he would ask his wife to hurry up their divorce, the proceedings having been started supposedly before we met. She was now also back with her boyfriend.

My mother was very good to me during this time. She of course had plenty of experience in these matters so managed to help me make some sense of the mess I had got myself into. It was good to talk to her, feeling she was not judging me. This was a time in my life when my mother came up trumps.

Robert was calling every day, saying he was very soon going to be divorced and our life would start anew. This proved difficult, as Robert's wife was now suddenly very distraught and wanted to get back with him again. She now did not want a divorce after all and started fighting for him. It would not be appropriate for me to write the details of this episode. It is sufficient to say that it was not an easy time for any of us. I felt sorry for all of us.

Several times over the proceeding months, Robert would visit, insisting that the following week I should come to Rome as he would have a house ready for us to move into, as his divorce was imminent. At the last moment, he would call and say the house had fallen through or some other excuse.

CHAPTER 15

1975. BACK IN ROME

By the time I was seven months pregnant, I flew to Rome with the promise that he had found us a house. I arrived in Rome to find no house, only a hotel room. By then, I was thoroughly fed up. I was left alone in the hotel whilst he went back to his house to "look after his boys". I just felt numb most of the time. I was in a strange country, just about to give birth and homeless. Thank goodness I had God in my heart, who I still managed to communicate with throughout this very difficult time. Somehow, a house by the sea just outside Rome became available, where we finally managed to make a life for ourselves. Robert's wife went back to the boyfriend she'd had, before Robert met me!

Living by the seaside was wonderful, in the small quaint village of Fregene. We started living there early August 1975. I spoke no Italian and had no friends nearby, but silence as ever was my friend, as was my love for God. I enjoyed getting the nursery ready, spending my time looking after the house and having lovely dinners ready in the evening.

One weekend, a month before Natasha was born, we had a bad car accident. One man died in the car that had driven into us, with horrific injuries to the other passengers in his car. I suffered from concussion and was rushed into hospital, fearing that I would give birth any moment. Robert suffered severe whiplash and was in pain for a long time.

Me Robert and Natasha 1976

CHAPTER 16

1975. NATASHA IS BORN

A month later, Natasha was born, a healthy beautiful baby. When I arrived back from the hospital, Robert had decked the house with 100 red roses.

But there was one thing missing; the marriage certificate, as Robert's divorce had not come through yet. One day after the birth, I slid into a silent depression for a while. This was the worst scenario I could have found myself in. More than anything, I had wanted to have a husband with a legal marriage behind me, for our baby's sake, more than for mine.

It was a mixed time of joy and challenges living by the seaside, being very isolated, with no possibility of getting help with Natasha. I had to manage the best I could with a new-born baby, and manage I did. Except when Robert's boys came for weekend visits; then the house would be in uproar. They were like wild children with no discipline. Lovely children, but difficult. They were sweet with Natasha, but I constantly had to keep an eye on them. I got so stressed that, after a few months, I lost my ability to breast feed her. She was crying and crying, and I had no idea she was starving. I walked down to the little chemist in the village, and the nice lady there told me that I probably needed to get some milk formula. So back I staggered with all sorts of bottles, including a milk formula, and started Natasha on that, much to my sorrow. But this did the trick. Soon, she was quiet and content, never giving me another moment of worry.

When Natasha was 3 months old, Robert had to go on an East Asian tour for his company. He insisted that I come with him and bring Natasha. We travelled to many countries.

In Bangkok, I bumped into Roman Polanski,

who was staying in the same hotel as us. It was so good to see him again. He told me that he was pleased things had worked out for me, when initially he and Gene Gutowski had doubts when they'd met Robert. In fact, after having read the letter that Gene wrote to me, when I had just left my mother's house to move to Rome, saying how worried he was about me, it is pretty evident that they were doubtful if Robert was the right man.

After Bangkok, we arrived in Taiwan. Natasha got a high fever and was rushed into hospital. I spent the night with her there, but thankfully she recovered, and we continued our journey.

We arrived in Singapore and booked into the famous Raffle Hotel. I had a peaceful week of recovering with Natasha, loving every moment with her in this beautiful hotel.

When we got back to Rome, it was evident that something was up with Robert's work. He had an Italian partner, and something was going wrong with their partnership. Apparently, some money was missing from the company. Natasha was 11 months old when Robert and his partner parted ways. We now had to rethink our lives.

Life in Italy was wonderful, but impractical. Robert's boys came to visit us every weekend, but they were a handful. They had never really settled into their school in Italy and had nervous temperaments. I decided it might be best for us all to move to England. I had another trust fund that was about to mature, which would help us afford a down payment on a house. So that was what we did.

Our first house in Guildford 1976

CHAPTER 17

1976. LIFE BEGINS IN ENGLAND AGAIN

Being back in England was energising for me. I knew the boys would do well there and thankfully found a good boarding school for them not too far away from our new home. Robert managed to get a good job quite quickly in London. I bought us a lovely house in Guildford and set about renovating it. Nine months later, it was ready, so I decided to put it on the market. I made a huge profit and with it bought us a stunning old manor house in another part of Surrey. It was such fun

Cowshot Manor 1977

doing up this beautiful old house. The boys were doing well at school and Natasha was thriving. We had nice friends and life was as good as it could be. During this time, Robert would ask me when we were going to get married, but I decided after a lot of thought that I just could not find it in my heart to say "I do" to a man who had lied to me on so many occasions. One day, I took myself off to my solicitor's office and officially deed-polled my name to Robert's surname. I came home that evening and placed the official papers on the table. There was nothing more to be said.

Even though we appeared to be a happy family to the outside world, there was an undercurrent of unease for me. Robert had started up a company in Nigeria, and I was doing my best to help him with his business. We employed a chauffeur. We also employed a young girl from the Seychelles Islands, whom we had met when we were on holiday there, to help in the house. When she arrived at our home, she was continually sick, until eventually we found out she was pregnant. I booked her into a private hospital, where she gave birth to a baby girl. For a few months, I looked after her and her baby. Later, she was to repay me with a cruel twist of fate.

One of the things that made me uneasy during this time was that Robert would not pay the household bills, which was his responsibility. A few times, the bailiffs would appear, but somehow, I managed to make them go away with the promise that I would make sure the bills were paid. It usually happened when Robert was away in Nigeria; he was often gone for weeks at a time. Robert's younger brother, Jos, who was working in Scotland, would come and stay periodically and was sympathetic to the stress I was under, always wondering who was at the front door coming to take our possessions for unpaid bills. He was my rock during this time. It was not for long though, as Robert got jealous when he found an inscription in a book Jos had given me, therefore would not allow him to come to the house again.

THE TAPPING INCIDENT

One weekend, I noticed that Robert had invited a man I had never met before into our home. They spent a lot of time in the study. Robert said he was having a new stereo system installed there. I felt a bit uneasy about this man but was polite, asking him if he needed a cup of tea or anything to eat, as they had spent many hours getting this so-called stereo system put in place.

Monday morning, after Robert had gone to work and our chauffeur had taken Natasha to school, there was a knock on the front door. When I looked out the window, it was the same man who had been in the house over the weekend. I asked him what he wanted. He said he needed to speak to me urgently. I said I could not let him in but for him to tell me through the window what he had to say. He told me that he had not slept all night, as he felt I was a good person and I needed to know that my husband had got him to install a bugging system on our phone. To prove it, he told me to go into the study and follow the lead behind the phone, which was now plugged into a tape-recorder. I found it and came back to the window and thanked him profusely.

It was evident that Robert wanted to catch me out on something, which, if I had not been told about the bugging devise, might have compromised a very important person I was speaking to on the phone. When Robert got back from work that evening, I sweetly greeted him and asked him to come into the study. I went behind his desk, bent down, picked up the tapping recorder, placed it on the desk, and for the first and last time in my life, hit a man across the face. He quickly walked out of the room.

Shortly after this incident, coming back from shopping, I went into the kitchen to place my groceries. There I found my husband's office chauffeur and our maid sitting at the kitchen table talking. It was then that another bombshell was dropped into my lap. The chauffeur announced that he had something to tell me that might interest me. He said he had just come back from taking my husband to the airport and dropped off a Miss Julia as well. He added that this had been going on for some months. This was not the first time I had been made aware that Robert was having an affair. I had turned a blind eye up until now. Somehow, this felt different.

I was right. When I confronted Robert about this Miss Julia, he told me she meant nothing to him. But the affair continued, and by Christmas, I'd had enough. We decided to have a trial separation. Robert took the boys skiing in Switzerland to think about our situation, but actually was staying with Julia and her parents in an apartment they had rented in St Moritz.

Natasha, the chauffeur, the maid, and I were left penniless at home. That was a strange Christmas to say the least. To make Christmas a bit more bearable, I bought them all Christmas presents on our joint

Harrods card, which Robert tried to use against me, unsuccessfully, during a court case we had later on.

Soon after Robert got back from Switzerland, he got our maid to sign a piece of paper to say I was having an affair with our chauffeur. He paid her £200 for her trouble. That night, he proceeded to beat me up in the dining hall, because he had decided he was distraught that I might be having an affair. Little did I know at the time that Julia was now pregnant with his child and pushing for him to leave me, so he could marry her! **The eighth step towards FORGIVENESS.**

I intuitively knew that the time had come to leave and start life anew. I consulted a lawyer about how to proceed with the separation, as well as selling our beautiful home. I soon found out that Robert had forged my signature at our bank, managing to get loans on our house. Most of my money and a lot of hard work on the previous house had paid for our beautiful manor, as well as my hard work doing this house up to a high standard, which had trebled in value since it was bought. I now found to my horror it was almost worthless on paper, as a huge debt was owed to our bank.

Robert decided to stay in London for a few months while I put our manor on the market. It was a miserable time for me. I used to get silent calls late at night, which was very disturbing. Twice the police were called in so the phone number could be changed, but it persisted right up until I left our home. The police had no doubt who was trying to frighten me! **Ninth step towards FORGIVENESS.**

The day dawned when I had to close the door on the beautiful manor I had lovingly done up and called home for the past three years. It had trebled in value, but my lawyer was only able to get a few thousand pounds secured for me, plus maintenance for our daughter. The rest of the proceeds for the sale of our house went on the overdraft for Robert's bad business deals in Nigeria, or whatever else he had spent our money on.

The only thing I would like to add is that I think I have a deep understanding of why Robert behaves as he does. He grew up as a young child in a Japanese concentration camp in Indonesia and had a really tough time there. Under the circumstances he has done well, and he is, underneath it all, a good man.

I have a special saying that goes like this: "At the core of every human being, they are pure, whole, and innocent."

I tried the best I could over the preceding years to be friends with Robert, his wife, and their three lovely children, for the sake of my daughter's happiness. It was not always easy, as no maintenance was forthcoming for Natasha. I remember being sure when I lived with Robert that the maintenance agreed between his ex-wife and himself was always paid on time for her and their two boys.

Our last Christmas together 1981

Natasha with Jeremy Lloyd 1982

CHAPTER 18

1982. A NEW LIFE BEGINS IN LONDON

I decided to move to London and put my daughter into a good private school in Kensington. I found a suitable flat for us and got a mortgage. Soon I found a job selling luxury apartments, alongside looking after my darling girl. It was good to be free, no longer burdened with lies and deceit.

It was not easy for Natasha to see her mother and father no longer together. She loved us both equally and

Natasha with Captain Beaky Toys

suffered from the split. She also suffered when Robert and Julia decided to keep her after a weekend visit with them. It took me weeks to get her back, and then it was only by kidnapping her that I got her back.

JEREMY LLOYD

To get Natasha back, I had the help of her headmistress and some dear friends of mine, who also had a daughter in Natasha's class. We arrived at the school one hour early, so as not to cause a scene when Natasha was due to be picked up by Robert, and drove to my friend's home. There sitting waiting for us was Jeremy Lloyd, the actor/writer, who had recently had success with some children's books called "Captain Beaky" that Natasha adored. They immediately struck up a friendship. Jeremy started larking about, making us all laugh. Before he left, he signed a Captain Beaky book for her, which I have kept as a treasure. The inscription reads thus: "For Natasha at six, from Jeremy with love and a nice hug from your lovely Mama. May 1982."

For a few days, Natasha was a bit depressed about the way things were turning out with her father and Julia, who was by then 5 months pregnant with their first child. It must have been very confusing for her, but we settled back into our routine, which we had always enjoyed. I managed to get a restraining order on Robert, until we got a court order to say that if he was granted visiting rights again, he had to return Natasha at the allocated time. But I never really trusted him, feeling nervous until Natasha was safely back in my care.

During this rough time, Jeremy came to visit us regularly and always made Natasha laugh. He spoilt her with all the Captain Beaky stuffed animals, which she kept for years. I can honestly say that Jeremy was a bit of a lifesaver during those days. We became good friends, and I a sounding board for some of the problems he was going through.

About a year later, the phone rang late one night; it was Jeremy saying, "I think I'm dying." I rushed over to his Mews house just opposite Clarence House in Piccadilly. He did not look well, so I called an ambulance to come immediately. I went out into the street to see if the ambulance had arrived and saw the guard keeping watch at the gate of Clarence House, where the Queen mother lived. The guards are not allowed to speak to the public, but I shouted to him, "Jeremy is ill, and I have called an ambulance. When you see it coming, please direct it into the Mews." He threw up his thumb and nodded.

Jeremy was in hospital for a good week, and I went to see him every day. I called all his nearest and dearest, including his second wife, Joanna Lumley. What a truly special person she is. I really like her. It is a shame they did not stay together, as it would have helped Jeremy so much with his life.

Me in English Church Copenhagen 1986

CHAPTER 19

1985. WHO AM I?

Over the next year, I worked hard and somehow managed to give Natasha and myself a good life. Now that I had more time to myself, I began to take a serious look at who I really was. For so long, I had been living in all these dramas, just existing from day to day, coping the best I could. I always had this inner feeling of peace and happiness, but outwardly the world seemed a strange and difficult place to negotiate. I started to read books that opened up my heart and true spirit. It felt like discovering a whole new existence.

There were still dramas unfolding, relationships I had to experience and go through, but somehow, I now had a deeper understanding that life is full of ups and downs; it is how we *deal* with these events that is important. Even in my darkest moments, through sexual abuse, lies, and betrayals, I remained hopeful, willing to see the best in people, regardless of whether they were showing me their worst side. We go through life discovering the truth of who we really are. Soon the distractions become a distant memory, with the glory of life opening up for us in the simplest of ways. I started to open up my heart by practicing being supremely grateful for what I did have. Another thing that gave me joy was helping anyone who needed it.

During this time, I was introduced to a man through some Turkish friends of mine, whose apartment I had interior designed. He was very impressed with my work and shortly after we set up a joint property business. The company bought a beautiful house in Edward Square, Kensington, close to Natasha's school. I spent 6 months doing it up, enjoying every moment. I was still able to maintain Natasha in all that she needed to be a well-educated young lady, although still no child support from her father was forthcoming. As the house in Edward Square was nearing its refurbishment, it was becoming increasingly clear that my business partner was falling in love with me. Unfortunately, I was unable to reciprocate, although if I had married him, I would not have had to worry about money for the rest of my life!

But then I have always fallen in love with the soul of a person, rather than outside trappings. I firmly believe that time is speeding up and the reason why we fall in love with various souls is to complete a circle of remembrance from previous lives. How else do you know almost the minute you meet someone that they feel so familiar? Your heart starts murmuring memories from the past that have to either be relived or concluded.

During my time in Edward Square, I met the sweetest young Iranian man, quite a few years younger than myself. He turned out to be one of my dearest loves, for sure an ancient soul I had to meet again. He pursued me for 6 months before I relented and we went on a date. We spent a happy year together until he decided he wanted to marry me. But his family were not amused, although they adored me. We had spent several holidays together on their yacht, sailing around the Greek islands. They also came to my home for dinner parties. It was very hard breaking up with D. as we got on so well together. I was just about to turn 40. If I was 40, it must have been 1988.

Us 3 sisters 1983.

Party with friends 1985

CHAPTER 20

1988. TAKE ROBERT TO COURT

After many years, keeping Natasha in the manner she was accustomed to, working and also trying to have a bit of a social life, I decided to take Robert to court, as I still had not received a penny from him in child support, since we had parted. After the court hearing, Robert was ordered to pay a big backlog of child support, as well as school fees. But to my dismay, he made himself bankrupt, so I never got a penny. Making himself bankrupt was not a hardship for Robert, as his wife was an extremely wealthy woman. Throughout Natasha's childhood, I never got a penny and had to do the best I could whilst paying for her education, extra lessons, food, clothes, holidays, etc. **The tenth step towards FORGIVENESS.**

Shortly after the court hearing, I went to Italy for a VIP wedding with a friend of mine. I was tired and run down, so I contracted pneumonia and had to spend two weeks in the Cromwell Hospital recovering. I remember late one night, I was particularly feverish and felt very low. I therefore decided to call Jeremy Lloyd for a bit of support. He answered the phone in a sleepy voice. I said it was me; I was in hospital with pneumonia and felt as if I was dying. He said, "Well, then, you are in the best place" and hung up! So much for friendship, after all I had done for him. I never spoke to him again after that incident. But I did hear later, from a friend, that he felt bad for not being supportive whilst I was ill.

It took me a while to recover from my brush with death. This was also the year Natasha finished at her private school in London. I sold my company, which was the house we lived in, at a great price. Dustin Hoffman had come to view it twice, which was such a treat, as on the second visit it was just him and myself sitting in the kitchen talking about the film business. But he didn't buy it in the end. After the sale, I moved to Wiltshire to do up an old barn I'd bought to be near Natasha, who had decided to go to boarding school there. Two years later, when Natasha's school folded, we moved back to London. I doubled my money on the sale of the barn. It was good to be back in London again.

I bought a beautiful flat in Kensington. Natasha was to complete the rest of her education in a crammer school for rich kids, not fare from our new home. What a mistake that was. So many nasty things happened during this time, with Natasha's character changing drastically. It was sad for me to see how she began to behave, I suppose to keep up with peer pressure. She became very aggressive towards me when I would not allow her to go out to night clubs or stay out late. It amazed me that the children she was in class with, most of them from rich, important families, would harass me by ringing my front door late at night, then running away, or I would wake up in the morning and find eggs thrown at my windows.

It was decided that Natasha should leave this school, as the drug use was rampant amongst these rich kids. For a while, she went to live with my younger sister in Scotland. There she was unhappy, so back she came to London, but slightly more calm than when she had left. Maybe mummy wasn't so bad after all! I sent her to another school, which she hated.

Every summer holiday, I used to take Natasha to Club Med, sometimes even during the Easter holidays. It was a perfect place for us as she would make lots of friends there, enjoying herself without having to be around boring Mum too much. When Natasha was 18, she was headhunted by Club Med and got a job as a dancer in their evening shows whilst looking after the Kids Club during the day. So began a wonderful life for her, traveling to many exotic countries and islands. She was happy and I was relieved that she had managed to find a good job, where drugs were not tolerated. She met her husband at Club Med a few years later, and they now have three beautiful children.

Top: The Barn Wiltshire 1987.
Below: The Barn done up 1988

Natasha in Mother's
ball gown

CHAPTER 21

1990. ANOTHER BIG TRAUMA

Yet another trauma was on its way, which caught me by surprise. My mother called one day to say that she wanted to invite me for lunch in the countryside. Just the two of us for some quality time together. We drove down to Kent and stopped off for lunch in a cosy pub. Afterwards, we went for a walk and found a lovely little church. A service was about to start, which we decided to attend. There were very few people at the service, so we were asked to come and sit in the choir pews.

In came the vicar, who proceeded to sit opposite to where we were sitting. I started to get a very uneasy feeling. I took a side glance at my mother, saw she had donned her famous sunglasses and scarf, realized what she had led me into and nearly fainted. For one whole hour, I had to sit opposite my *real* father. This was the first time I had laid eyes on him. I felt utterly sick and deceived. After the service was over, I ran down the aisle, out into the cold night air. I was shivering violently. We drove back to London in silence.

That night, when I got back to my flat, was another dark night of my life. I felt so utterly let down. A deep cloud descended upon me. I had been through so many things in my life, but this was a complete violation. Somehow, I managed to get through the night. How I got over this shock I simply can't remember, but I did, probably with the help from You know Who! I spoke to no one of this event, I just got on with life. I did not speak to my mother for a long time afterwards. Slowly, forgiveness descended in my heart, and I began talking to her again. Maybe life just brings us a series of events that give us the gift and grace to forgive at the deepest level? Or maybe I am just getting very good at this forgiveness business?

By then, I had moved on from the property business, becoming a PA to the owner of an insurance company in London. I met a film producer through mutual friends, and after a while, we started dating. Little did I know that this man was so obsessed with the divorce of his previous wife that it had made him a bit unstable. Eventually, I decided that I could not cope with his endless pursuit of the court case he had made against his ex-wife's lawyer, who had become involved with his ex-wife during their divorce, so I decided to finish our friendship. He became very bitter and called up my employer's wife and told her that I was having an affair with her husband. This was an utter lie and made me very sad. It also made my boss very sad, as his wife took the allegations seriously, demanding I resign from the company or else! I decided that enough was enough and left, with, I might add, a sizable compensation that my solicitor managed to get for me.

CHAPTER 22

1993. REIKI AND HEALING ENTERS MY LIFE

The above incident again opened up a new life for me. You see how sometimes difficult circumstances can be a blessing in disguise? Well, this was one of them. As the saying goes, one door closes and another one opens. I now had time to think about what my next move was going to be. My daughter was working abroad, so my expenses were halved. I decided to embark on a new way of life.

My love for God was growing by the day. I had such an urge to finally find the truth of who I was and why I was here in the first place. My hunger for self-enquiry was growing by the hour. It felt as if a very exciting time in my life was about to unfold. Most people might have panicked, but I got ready to embrace the unknown, with certainty that this was going to be a good outcome, maybe even the purpose of my life's journey.

First, I embarked on a healing course with the Athenian Society in London. We had to wear white overcoats whilst healing and were not allowed to touch people with cancer. I decided after a week this course was not for me. I then went to the Body, Mind and Spirit Fair in the Victoria Horticulture Hall, London. I had never been to such an event before. As I entered the Hall, a smell of incense so ancient greeted me. I wandered around and came to a healing stand with REIKI written above it. I thought I would try that and booked an appointment for a healing session. Whilst waiting for my Reiki treatment, I walked about the Hall, enjoying every moment, looking at beautiful crystal stands, and bought a few Tibetan singing bowls, which I still use today.

The appointed time came for my Reiki treatment. I was asked to lie down on a treatment table. The Australian husband and wife who were giving the treatment, one standing by my head, the other at my feet, proceeded to give me the Reiki healing. Before I knew where I was, my spirit had been transported up through the roof of the building and taken to a place that felt very peaceful. In this place of beauty and peace, I was shown a vast amount of people sitting at an oval table looking at me. After a while, I asked what I was doing there and was told that I was being realigned. In fact, I was being re-tuned so that my vibration level would be vibrating at a higher frequency. I was also asked by the person sitting at the head of the table if I was willing to become a healer and help humanity heal themselves. There was no hesitation when I answered, "YES." (I later discovered that Astral Travelling allows us to realize that we are not *only* the body, therefore are able to alter our vibrations.)

The next thing I knew, I was awake and being asked to get off the treatment table. Dazed, I got off, then told this lovely Australian couple what had happened. They were visibly shaken themselves, as they related to me that they had also been transported to witness the event. They asked me to join them at their next Reiki healing course, which I gladly accepted.

MY MEETING WITH MOTHER MEERA

A whole new life opened up for me. I loved the Reiki healing course and took to it immediately. The following week, the Australian couple were going to visit Mother Meera in Germany and asked me to come with them.

Mother Meera is a spiritual personality who is not a teacher in the conventional sense. She is an embodiment of the Divine Feminine, the Divine Mother on earth. She is not a Guru who takes disciples. She has no interest in conversion or changing anyone's beliefs. She has come to prepare and cleanse world consciousness for us to be ready for transformation to a higher evolution. She calls down the Light of the Supreme Consciousness. She is preparing humanity to become open to this Light, so the Divine life can be manifested on Earth. She suggests that, on the spiritual path, there is no competition with all other Saints.

From Mother Meera's book *Answers*: "It is not necessary to believe in me. If you are sincere to your Guru, Master, or to the Divine, it is enough, and I will strengthen your faith. If you need me, I will help you in whatever path you may follow. For me, there is no difference. All paths lead to the same goal, that is … to realize the Divine."

The experience with Mother Meera was extraordinary. When I met her, I felt as if my heart and chakras were given a good clean up in preparation for a new life. I felt myself throwing away all that was binding me to my past life story. I started firmly believing in the best, the positive, to draw the highest potentials into my life. When I had thought that all was lost, it was simply the beginning of improving myself that was needed. I started to fully believe in myself and learnt that it is always possible and necessary to start again. Now I could look higher, dream higher. I could renew my hopes of a better life. Life was calling me, inviting me to a new adventure, a new journey, a new challenge.

One month later, I met Mata Amritanandamayi, often known as Amma, who is an Indian Hindu spiritual leader, guru and humanitarian, who is revered as the "Hugging Saint" by her followers; then a month after that, I met the Dalai Lama.

After my meeting with Mother Meera, I did my second course in Reiki healing. It was during this weekend that one of the participants, by the name of Susan, gave me a book on Sri Sathya Sai Baba (*Divine Memories of Sathya Sai Baba*, by Diana Baskin), as well as a picture of Him and some holy ash from His Ashram in India. A while later, during my meditation in front of Mother Meera's picture, I experienced to my astonishment her eyes opening and closing. I asked her inwardly what she wanted to convey to me. Clearly, I heard her say, "It is time for you to connect with your lifelong Guru. Read the book that Susan gave you!" I did just that. It was not long after reading this book I was on a plane to visit the great Avatar Sri Sathya Sai Baba. More of that later.

I had put aside a room in my flat and invited friends to come for a Reiki healing. Very soon, I was getting good results. Then I decided to do a Reflexology course at Barnes Hospital. After a year, I was also qualified with a degree in anatomy and physiology. Many people came to me for healing. I soon had a client list that included many famous people.

One particular young lady I was treating was the daughter of the owner of Asprey in London. Her mother, Elizabeth, was dying of cancer. She was in intensive care in the London Clinic. One day, she came to me and said she'd had a dream that I would heal her mother and that I was to come to the London Clinic with her right away. After much protesting, she finally managed to persuade me to go with her.

We arrived and were ushered outside her mother's room. I was decked in a plastic apron, shoes and mask. Then I was led into the room, where her mother lay in a coma, looking the colour of death. I was left alone to get on with it. I sat myself at the end of her bed, was guided to place my hands at the bottom of her feet, after applying the sacred ash, that I had previously been given by Susan, and started to pray. After a while, I opened my eyes and saw a pink flush creep over her face, starting from her neck. A minute or so later, the lady opened her eyes and asked who I was. I said my name was Leonora, that I was a friend of her daughters. She asked me if I was an angel. I said, "No." I left the room somehow knowing that the lady would be all right, and she was!

CHAPTER 23

1994. A DIFFICULT MEETING

One day in 1994, I got a call from my mother to say that my biological father's wife had passed away. This had given her the opportunity to get in touch with him again. They'd met for lunch and rekindled their friendship. My mother asked me if I would like to meet my father. I said I would think about it. Eventually, my mother persuaded me to meet him at his home, but she insisted that she also would be coming along.

The day arrived, and we drove to his house. I don't remember much from the meeting, except that my father was not very warm and more interested in talking about his own life. This has always been a bit of a puzzle to me. I have still not come up with an answer as to why I felt very little when I met him. I never saw him again, but my mother continued her friendship with him until he passed away in 1996.

Looking back on this meeting with my biological

father and why I felt very little emotion, I imagine it was because he had never shown any interest in me whatsoever. By the time he passed away, he had never mentioned me to his son, my half-brother, and left me nothing in his will. He was probably embarrassed about the situation and didn't know how to handle it.

This was when I learnt once again to go beyond forgiveness and land in a place where it does not disturb my equilibrium.

This is what going **beyond forgiveness** means. We have to learn that to forgive a dramatic situation or event, it needs first to be understood in the mind, then the heart, to arrive peacefully in the soul, where there resides only Love and Peace.

CHAPTER 24

1994. MEETING JACK TEMPLE

I first met Jack Temple at a Body Mind and Spirit Fair in August 1994. I had attended a lecture he was giving there. It immediately struck me what an amazing, dynamic man he was, at the ripe old age of 77. At the time, I had tennis elbow, which was causing me a lot of pain, so after the lecture, I decided to see if it would be possible to get an appointment with him.

As I rushed towards his stand, where he was selling his potions, I saw him ahead of me, with a trail of people following him, probably wanting an appointment as well. I was just a few feet from him when he spotted me. He looked me intensely in the eyes and said, "Martha, where have you been?" I looked behind me to see if he was talking to someone else, but no, it was me he had intended to pose the question to.

Luckily for me, this offered an opportunity to speak with him immediately, as he bypassed everyone else. He gave me his card and asked me to call his clinic in the morning.

This I duly did and secured an appointment with him the following day. That was also strange, as I had heard that it would normally take weeks, even months to get a much-coveted appointment with him. He was in great demand, treating members of our Royal Family, as well as other famous people, with his huge reputation of being able to heal people's ailments.

I arrived in Byfleet, Surrey, where his clinic was situated. There were many people waiting to see him. As I announced myself to his secretary, she informed me that I would be his next patient, as per his instructions.

As I entered his office, I was taken aback by the unique look of it! Hundreds of bottles lined the walls with all kinds of fossils, crystals and herbs inside them. He motioned me to sit down, came to stand by me and started swinging his pendulum over me. After a while, he looked up and his face was shining. "I thought so," he beamed. "Your name was Martha, and we worked together in the pyramids 5000 years ago. Welcome back into my life." My first thought was that this was what he said to all the ladies he saw, but no, he was serious, and I had to take him at his word.

I had just started dating the famous writer/

director Robert McKee. I met him at one of his writing courses in London. On the second day, during one of the breaks, Bob came up and started talking to me. It was one of those strange moments again when I knew he was an old soul I had known before. After the course finished, we had a drink in the bar and spent hours talking. It was an easy, uncomplicated flow. At the time, Bob had frozen thumb, which really annoyed him, as it hindered him using his typewriter for his work. I offered to give him healing, and so it was that he ended up in my flat the following evening for dinner and a healing session. I can still see me sitting next to him on the sofa, holding his hand and sending healing to his frozen thumb. After his thumb unfroze itself, Bob looked at me in astonishment. After that, we went on a few dates, then planned to go away on a holiday together. Bob even cut his hair shorter, as I had said I thought his hair looked a bit scruffy.

But Jack must have done some voodoo on Bob, because a few days later, after meeting Jack, I got a call from Bob, saying he could no longer see me! Instinctively, Jack must have known that I had no time for boyfriends for now, as I had much learning to do for my healing work.

Very soon, Jack and I began where we had left off and started working together. We traveled to many countries to dowse for herbs, crystals, as well as all kinds of tree barks, amongst other curious things, to bring back and harvest for curing the ills of his patients. One particular journey I remember with fondness was when we traveled to Morocco to find some remedies for patients waiting back in UK. We came to a market where Jack was busy dowsing around a stand full of crystals and skulls of small dead animals. The owner of the stall was eyeing me up, which was making me feel a bit uncomfortable. When Jack had selected what he needed, the owner asked if he could purchase me for forty camels! We laughed all the way back to the hotel and many times after that as well. We also traveled to Egypt to experience the time we had worked there together in the pyramids. I have three albums full of glorious pictures of our travels together.

Jack's unique way of healing was way ahead of his time. He used a silver pendulum with a green emerald in it (he had one made up for me as well, from the same emerald), identifying toxins, clearing the energy field around the body, applying homeopathic remedies to balance the patients' energies to encourage their own natural healing. He helped the lame to walk, the barren to conceive and the sad to smile. He was able to inflate lungs of children previously condemned to a life constricted by asthma. He was passionate about cell-renewal, as I myself have started to work with in these latter years of my healing practice.

As time went by, Jack's health kept improving after I got into the habit of giving him healing whenever I could. He had been very ill just before I met him. He trusted me implicitly, and I felt honoured as he had never let anyone give him healing before.

Jack was constantly striving to discover new ways to improve his healing methods. He would often use his wife as a test subject to try out a new treatment, then lo and behold a patient would arrive the next day who needed that exact treatment. This used to always surprise Jack, but at the same time, it would amuse him. Jack's wife had been struck by lightning one day when they were out on a picnic. Jack told me that he was sitting in the car and she had gone to place some rubbish in a bin. All of a sudden, a huge bolt of lightning came crashing down and struck his wife. Jack was unharmed in the car, but his wife was not well from that day onwards. It was in fact this incident that lead Jack to become a dowser, to find a cure for his wife.

Jack also encouraged me to study Iridology at Queen Elizabeth Hospital in London, a course which took a year. I would then be able to take pictures of his patients' eyes before his treatments, then again 6 months later to see if there had been an improvement. In this way, he would be able to show that his treatments worked. Iridology is a way of looking at the iris of the eye to determine imbalances in the body.

Another interesting thing Jack and I did was to build huge Stone Circles for healing. We went to France and stayed with a girlfriend of mine, who led us to the place where some beautiful lavender was growing. Jack dowsed for it, declaring that it was perfect to put in amongst the stones in the Stone Circle in the grounds of his clinic. Patients used to sit on special chairs in front of each stone and get healing, transported from the Main Stones, which emanated energy harnessed from the Sun, Moon and Stars.

Sarah, Duchess of York, wrote a Foreword in Jack's first book, *The Healer*: "Jack's work is unique. It means he has to take on criticism from medical and other people, who disagree with what he does. I believe wholeheartedly in him, but, as always with anything different from the norm, people are often prejudiced rather than open-minded. If there were not people around like Jack Temple, who are prepared to stand up for what they believe in and fight for it, where would the world be!"

Jerry Hall wrote an introduction for Jack's second book, *Medicine Man*: "Going to Jack Temple was a life-enhancing experience. He cured me, my sister, my mother and my children of all our ailments. He is a genius worker."

One day, Jerry Hall came to see me to have her eyes photographed for Jack. I was the first person to know that she was pregnant with her last child with Mick Jagger. She did not want Mick or the press to know, so we kept it secret for a while; it was just her and me who knew. Jerry was a lovely person to know, and I wish her well always.

I shall never forget when Cherry Blair came to see Jack, as one of her legs had swelled up. After one treatment from Jack, her leg went down to normal size. This was enough to get her interested in seeing Jack many times for other treatments.

When Tony and Cherry's last child, Leo, was born, there was a big hue and cry over the MMR vaccination. Jack was of the opinion that it could cause autism in some children. He had successfully taken out the residual of the vaccine in many children who were showing signs of autism, who had been 'cured' after his treatment. This is well documented in Jack's books. So it went without saying that the Blairs were very worried about giving Leo the MMR. The press got wind of this and demanded that the Prime Minister should show support for the rest of the country's parents and have his child vaccinated. All I can say is that late one night, Jack was summoned to 10 Downing Street; but he swore me to secrecy, so I can't tell you why he went!

Jack Temple's office 1995

My office

I have found a cure!

CHAPTER 25

1995. ENTER THE ROYAL FAMILY

It was shortly after I started working with Jack that Sarah, Duchess of York, came to see him, as well as on several occasions, Prince Andrew, who would turn up at the clinic with her or on his own. I have to make one thing clear: I am not divulging, in this respect, anything that has not already been written in the press. I have so many secrets inside me that have been told to me in confidence over many years, and I would never dream of breaking any that has been entrusted to me.

Sarah and Andrew did not make it a secret that they were seeking Jack's help. He soon introduced them to me, and a strong friendship formed in no time. I used to see Prince Andrew at Sunningdale Park most Sunday afternoons, which was their marital home, given to them by the Queen as a wedding present. After their separation, Sarah moved into a rented house of her own. I used to go there most Saturdays.

More often than not, Prince Andrew was also there, as well as Princess Diana, whose divorce came through on 28 August 1996. It is not often mentioned that Princess Diana was deeply supported by Sarah during the difficult time leading up to her divorce from Prince Charles. When I met Diana at Sarah's house, she was often sad, but on occasions, we would end up in Sarah's bedroom, watch tennis and have a good laugh.

It goes without saying that Sarah was also reeling from her own life experiences. She had married her handsome prince in July 1986. They were so in love. But by 1992 they'd separated, as Andrew was always traveling. It is difficult to understand how hard it was for Sarah to hardly ever see her husband, who was always away on naval duties, with Sarah having to look after their big home and two children, while fulfilling many Royal duties, including her own charity work. She was always pushing herself to do more and more as she struggled with low self-esteem and wanted desperately to be liked by everyone.

If you read her autobiography, *My Story*, which incidentally is a brilliant read, you will get to know her a lot better and how much she had to suffer, not only after her own parents' divorce, but also throughout her life, struggling to like herself. When the honeymoon period with the press was over, after her marriage to

Andrew, she had to endure the endless harassing and hurtful press, when in the beginning she was thought of as a breath of fresh air in the Royal Family.

Sarah eventually embarked on a relationship with John Bryan, who she trusted to start looking after her finance, as Andrew was never about. She had been struggling so much to cope with everything on her own that one cannot blame her for turning to someone who was offering support and a bit of comfort as well. That was also the year that the infamous photos of John Bryan kissing Sarah's toes by the pool of the house they had rented for the summer holidays in France appeared in the tabloid. Beatrice was four and Eugenie was two.

It has recently been revealed by John that it was a completely innocent day of playing around the pool with the children, while Sara pretended to be Cinderella, who had lost her shoe and John was trying to find it, kissing her toe when he had. In Sarah's autobiography, she has also mentioned that episode. Those tabloids, they really are a menace.

But later, John Bryan cut the knife in deeply when he sold a story to the tabloids that he'd once had sex with Sarah when she was on the phone to Andrew. She was devastated and hurt beyond words, as this was not the truth at all. Sarah has done a great job at forgiving left right and center. I truly admire her for her courage.

When I first met Sarah, she was still reeling from this scandal of the photos and the fact that her marriage had collapsed. But she felt there was no return. Somehow, throughout all the ups and downs, Andrew and Sarah have always remained friends, of which I am a witness.

They finally got divorced on 30 May 1996. I was seeing them both during this time, and there was definitely a sadness about them due to the finality of the beautiful dream they'd had at the beginning of their partnership, which had come to an end.

Their ability to maintain a good, solid relationship is testimony that they are soul mates. I remember the incident when Sarah apparently had been caught in a scam by a fake Sheikh to get paid cash for access to Andrew. In my heart, I knew this could not be true. Sure enough, the next day, I got a call from Andrew. He was devastated, saying to me, "Our Sarah would never do a thing like that." I totally agreed with him. The opinion of the matter was that the video interview had been tampered with, so it looked like this was what she meant, when what she had said was that if this man wanted to be introduced to Andrew, she could arrange it. The money was about another issue. I was not there, but I also know Sarah well enough to know that she would never intentionally want to embarrass or hurt Andrew.

2009

To my most special
and devoted, unique
and Amazing Leonora.
    Thank you for your
Purity, love and
golden Heart.
    Words are not enough
to explain my gratitude
    All my love Your Friend
Sarah xxx Always.

Letter from Sarah

CHAPTER 26

1996. ENTER PRINCESS DIANA INTO MY LIFE

It was not long before Princess Diana came to consult Jack as well. He treated her over twenty times. It was fascinating working with her. I must be the only person who has a huge blowup of the iris of her eyes, which was taken one weekend in Sarah's house, when Prince Andrew was there as well. My special iridology camera failed to click, whilst I tried desperately to get it to work, when Andrew said, "Leonora, let me try," and so it was that it was actually Andrew who took the photo! This, I realize now, was the universe wanting a witness to the fact that they are Princess Diana's eyes, which have copyright on them and will be given to her boys, if they would like them. And here they are!

Diana was very grateful for Jack and myself, helping her get more confidence in herself and get over her eating disorder, which we believed first stemmed from her troubled childhood. Her lack of understanding

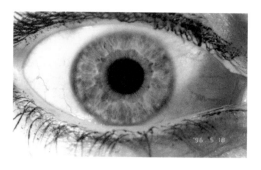

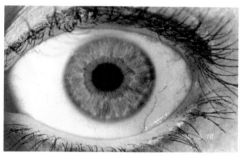

Iris of Princess Diana 1996 ©Leonora Vawn

of life with the Royal Family and constantly being chased by the press, after she married Prince Charles, about how difficult it was to cope with the ever-increasing public demand on her, also played a big role in her eating disorder. Jack gave Diana an amethyst crystal for her healing. She wrote such a sweet letter, thanking him, saying she would always treasure it.

Diana was also very paranoid during the last few years of her life. She was led to believe that there were spies in her midst, spying on her every move, shadowing and eavesdropping on her phone. She had difficulty trusting even her best friends. There were not many people that Diana trusted. She had always had a trusted friend in her sister, Jane, but when Jane's husband, Robert Fellows, became the Queen's Private Secretary in 1990, Diana became increasingly wary of confiding in her sister. This left Diana with few precious people she could air her deepest thoughts to, which was not a good place for her wellbeing to be in. At such a tender age of 19, she had so much thrown at her. She was undoubtedly in love with her husband, but as is well known, this turned out to be a marriage of convenience for Prince Charles rather than a marriage of Love. As he so famously said, "Whatever love is."

She unfortunately consulted several psychics after separating from Charles; they told her that her life was in danger. She would arrive at the clinic in tears, and Jack would get to work on her, clearing her brain and calming her down. Then he would call me in, if I was free, to talk to her, whilst he went out to the kitchen area to make us all one of his famous cups of Fortnum & Mason Keemun tea, lased with organic honey.

In 1995, Princess Diana's brother, Earl Charles Spencer, had been given some documentations by the BBC journalist Martin Bashir (that eventually proved to be fraudulent), which indicated that there were people out to get her. It has been discovered now, some 25 years later, that Bashir probably maneuvered Diana into believing this, by showing her the forged bank documents he had obtained by a BBC graphic designer, making her also to believe that staff close to her brother were being paid off for information about her. This encouraged her to do the Panorama Interview with Bashir. She was even concerned that Prince Charles would declare her insane and have her put away. She now started to distrust even those closest to her.

Diana's private secretary, Patrick Jephson (1988-1996), was also suggested by Bashir to be against her. He told her that Jephson was in league with Prince Charles' advisors, who was also paid to spy on her through security services, and that, for years, she had been betrayed by her worst enemies. Bashir also indicated gross allegations about other members of staff and her in-laws. For Bashir, it was a triumph of preparation, invention, opportunism and delivery that secured the covered Panorama interview with Princess Diana.

Diana made the historic Panorama interview with Martin Bashir on 5th November 1995, who had gained her trust because of the said forged documents to back up her theory that something was amiss. Diana felt, if she put the record straight on what was going on in her life, it would ease her fear of being 'bumped off', as she used to say. She was also worried she would be gagged from speaking out about how she felt she had been betrayed by the Royal Family in many ways. It was now or never to have her say. She wanted to fight back and show the world that she was a strong woman in her own right. The day before the infamous interview, Diana saw Jack and told him she was about to do something very important, which would have a big impact on her life, as well as Prince Charles and the rest of the Royal Family. He did several treatments on her to calm her nerves. The night of the Panorama Interview, Diana was cool, calm and collected.

Diana and Jack always had a sweet connection; she adored him and trusted him implicitly. He told Diana she was a great healer, and that made her happy. He also gave her an amethyst crystal for clearing negative energy and for protection. It amused them that they both had their birthdays on 1st July.

After Diana's divorce, when she lost her HRH, her mother did an interview and said how happy she was that Diana could now get on with her life in her own right. She had promised Diana that she would not do any interviews about her. Diana was furious and never spoke to her mother again. It was a déjà vu moment in Diana's life, as Diana's grandmother had gone against

Diana's mother during her divorce case, which lost her the custody of her children. Diana's mother also never spoke to her own mother again.

Recalling this has brought memories back to me. When I left Robert, my mother wrote to him, saying if ever he needed her, she would always be there for him. Disloyalty is a hard pill to swallow. But I forgave her.

Diana was very worried about the performance of her son Harry's work at school. She was worried that when it came to sit his exams for Eaton, where his brother William was at school, he would not pass them. Diana was determined that Harry would go there as well. She turned to Jack for help. In his unique way of treating, Jack devised a treatment for Harry to clear his brain. When he sat his entrance exam, he got in! Whether this was because of Jack's treatment we will never know.

In early 1997, Jack, Sarah and Diana flew in a helicopter up to Derbyshire to visit with the Psychic/Medium Rita Rodgers, who Sarah trusted implicitly. When Jack came back from this trip, he told me everything that had been said, and I was flabbergasted.

Later, Diana brought Dodi Al Fayed, who she was dating, to see Rita, after she had predicted that Diana would meet a man of foreign descent with the initial D in France on the water and that he would be connected with the film industry. Dodi had been so impressed by the prediction, he wanted to meet Rita in the flesh. When they met, she told Dodi to avoid France and not to change his limo driver for fear of an accident in a tunnel, words that were proved to be correct and retold by a friend of Dodi's in an interview. Rita told Jack later that she could not understand why she had not seen that Diana would be in the same car accident.

Then came that dreadful night, 31st August 1997, when our beautiful Princess Diana died in Paris, whilst the car she was in with Dodi went speeding along in a tunnel. Both Jack and I were in shock, as was the rest of the world. We had seen her only a few weeks earlier before she'd gone on her holiday with Dodi.

I was summoned to Sunning Hill Park to comfort Prince Andrew and the two small princesses. All were in deep shock. I arrived and was shown up to Prince Andrew's bedroom, where he was lying on his bed with one of his daughters in each arm. I shall never forget the look on the faces of the two sweet little princesses, their big eyes looking at me, asking if I thought "Duchy", as they used to call her, was now in heaven. I assured them she was, and they seemed satisfied with that. They asked me if I could give them some of my "angel dust", which was what they used to call the holy ash Vibhuti I used to carry with me in a tin with an angel on it, as it might make them feel better.

It is my belief that if Princess Diana had not done the Panorama Interview in 1995 and so incensed the Royal Family, she may not have lost her HRH title in her divorce settlement the following year, therefore would have had protection wherever she went, including Paris on that fateful night.

CHAPTER 27

1995. ENTER SRI SATHYA SAI BABA

He came to light the lamp of love in our hearts, to transform ourselves through enquiry as to who we are, finally bringing us to self-realization that will bring us Home.

Now comes truly the most significant time of my life, which changed the whole scenario. As I mentioned previously, I decided to read the book I was given on Sri Sathya Sai Baba one weekend in 1995. I read the book and was so moved and impressed that I found myself on a plane, bound for India a short while later, to meet this special Holy man. My friends and family alike were aghast that I was going alone to India. I had no idea or knowledge of where I was going. I just kept hearing this **VOICE** inside me, saying, "Trust me, I will look after you." The Voice sounded so familiar, as

I had heard it many times before; it always managed to access my higher self, where I felt safe and loved.

A few days before leaving my house for the airport, I had a phone call from a friend to say that some friends of his would look after me once I reached Bangalore. Again, I trusted and was duly met by a very nice couple, who took me to their home. They had heard a lot about me from our mutual friend, especially about the healing work I was doing and the good results it often produced. They wanted me to meet a group of doctors for lunch the next day to talk about my work. But I was adamant I had come to India to see Sai Baba, and I wanted to get there as soon as possible.

The following morning, my hosts graciously lent me their chauffeur, who would drive me the three hours it would take to reach Sai Baba's Ashram, Prasanthi Nilayam, Puttaparthi in South India. As I got into the car, they handed me a note, which, upon reading, as we sped on our way to Puttaparthi, read:

Sai Ram Mrs Shouri,
Please seat the bearer of this note.
Regards C. Sreenivas

My reaction to the note was the assumption that everyone needed a note to get into Sai Baba's Ashram.

What an amazing drive it was. I was all alone in India, being driven by a stranger to a place I knew very little about. The feeling in my heart was overwhelming. It was thumping more and more loudly as the miles were left behind and we neared the holy abode of 'The Living God'. As we entered the village of Puttaparthi, the wide road, leading to Sai Baba's Ashram, was flanked on either side by pink and blue buildings, which my driver told me were the colleges and hostels for the Sai students receiving education totally free of cost.

When I arrived, I booked myself into Sai Towers Hotel, then went across the road, entering a large gate into the Ashram. Many people were walking about in Indian-type clothes. The men were in white trousers and tops, the ladies in Saris or Punjabis. Luckily, I had an outfit on that was suitable. I handed in my note to the first official-looking person I could find and was told to go to the VIP gate. Well, that was a turn up for the books! *VIP entrance? What does that mean?* I wondered.

Before I could even contemplate my good fortune, I found myself being ushered into the large Temple Hall and was shown a seat in the first line on the ladies section. There must have been at least 20,000 people in the Temple. Shortly afterwards, Sai Baba in His shimmering orange robe entered. Within a minute He stood before me, smiled and said, "So you have come. Very happy." There was such beauty, such peace, such holiness about this God man. I felt so at home, so loved, so comfortable, as if it was the most natural thing in the world to sit crossed legged on the marble floor of this huge Temple in South India, being addressed so lovingly by Him. It seemed as if life stood still for an eternity. Then He walked on. That was when I heard the familiar Voice inside me again. "Did I not tell you I would look after you?"

The week sped by. I spoke to no one, except an Iranian lady, who looked after me for that week. (Dear Nooshin, who I was to meet again fourteen years later, just hours after Sai Baba had blessed my hands, indicating for me to start thinking about writing my life story.) Food became very irrelevant, as if my appetite had vanished, as if just being near Sai Baba was food enough. It certainly was for my soul!

Sai Baba did not speak to me again for the rest of that week, but gently and lovingly smiled at me as He walked past me every day, as I was always ushered to a place in first line! Often, I would hear Him talking to my innermost being as I sat contemplating my existence. One sentence I remember was this: "You are capable of loving many times, because you are the manifestation of love." This gave me comfort, as I had loved many times and wondered why. Although I can't remember too much of the time I spent there, Sai Baba must have been working on me in a profound way on my innermost being. I think He was getting me ready for the work He had planned for me in the future! But there was still a lot of finetuning to be done on my part as well. *What would have happened to me if my soul had not heard His call?*

Happy to be so close to Sai Baba

CHAPTER 28

1996. MY MEETING WITH KAYA GÜNATA

When I got back to UK, I could not get hold of enough books to read about Sai Baba. One day, my colleague, Jack Temple, got a call from an old friend of his, the amazing Turkish healer Kaya Günata. He wanted to invite Jack for dinner and asked him to bring someone with him and wondered if Jack knew who that person should be. I came along, and what a special evening it was to be introduced to Kaya. To meet a man who was so close and deeply involved with Sai Baba was such a blessing for me. We talked for hours about Sai Baba, whilst Jack sat listening. What was astounding about that evening was that Kaya gave both Jack and I a photo of Baba. I saw Jack put his photo in his pocket, but by the end of the evening, it was not to be found. Kaya had also given me a small packet of Vibhuti (holy ash), which years later, after having been put away empty in a draw, manifested a further amount of Vibhuti.

Kaya Günata with Stephen Turoff 1996

Kaya told us he had just come back from India, where he had been staying in Sai Baba's Ashram, as he and Victor Kanu did a lot of work together for Sai Baba in Africa. He had also gone in for an Interview. Kaya showed Sai Baba a detailed project for an ashram to be built in Turkey on land that he wanted to offer. Sai Baba manifested a green, emerald ring for him, told him that the time was not right, and that he would be called when it was.

In February 1997, I took Sarah, the Duchess of York, to see Sai Baba. We arrived in Bangalore and stayed there for a few days. I introduced Sarah to Dr Mathai, who is a holistic physician and homeopath, who I had met on my first trip to India. (He became famous after his meeting with Sarah, when the news hit the newspapers in India, as well as back in UK. With his newfound fame, he started a wonderful Holistic Health Centre in Whitefield just outside Bangalore, called Soukya, where King Charles and Queen Camilla now visit regularly.)

During our stay in Bangalore, in the beautiful Oberoi Hotel, I unfortunately never left my room, as I was constantly throwing up with suspected food poisoning. On the second day, there was a knock at my door, and a large vase with eighteen beautiful orange roses was delivered to me, but with no note. I asked who had sent them, but nobody owned up. I came to realize it was from Sai Baba, who was feeling sorry for me while I was being cleansed before I had my first Interview with Him!

We arrived in Puttaparthi with a few friends of ours in tow and drove to the car entrance gate of the Ashram, where we handed in our passports. We were told that Sai Baba was expecting us and were invited to stay in His VIP villa. How amazing was that! After we had dined on a most delicious lunch, with the food tasting as if it was made in heaven, we were ushered down to the Main Temple. We were given special seats by the gate, where Sai Baba enters the Temple. When He came in, as He passed us, smiling, asking us if we had enjoyed our lunch. He then moved on. After He had toured the Temple, on both the male and female side, He went into His Interview Room. A few minutes later, a lady named Mrs Mahadi came and told us to follow her, as we had been called for Interview. Later, she told me she was also a Reiki Master and that Sai Baba approved of this healing method. In fact, He had said to her that there should be Reiki practiced in every town in every country!

As we entered the Interview Room, Sai Baba was standing by the door to greet us. He told us to sit on the floor and asked if we were hot, then switched on a large fan. He proceeded to give us Vibhuti (holy ash). The feeling of love emanating from Him was infusing the room; it made everything seem as if it melted into being in another dimension.

His first question was directed to Sarah. He asked her how she was and what did she want.

She said, "Peace and happiness, Baba."

Again He asked her what she wanted.

This time, she said, "My children's health and happiness."

Sai Baba smiled at her and said, "I know what you want." With that, He made some circles with His hand and out of it came a gold cross studded with emeralds, hanging from a gold chain. (Later, Sarah told me that she had inwardly said, as we were being led to His

Interview Room, "Sai Baba, if you really are the Living God Leonora says you are, please give me a holy sign.") So this was the holy sign that demonstrated that there was to be no doubt in her mind, that He was the Living God.

Then Sai Baba turned His attention on me. He was sitting in His chair and asked me to come and sit by His feet. He patted me on the shoulder and said to everyone, "Very good woman, very good woman." With a sweet smile on His face, He followed it by saying, "But sometimes a little mad." At the time, it felt a bit embarrassing to hear this, but now it makes perfect sense. I think when we live unconsciously, we do many mad things without really thinking of the consequences. This is why Sai Baba has been the greatest of teachers, constantly impressing on me that to live consciously is the only option.

Whilst sitting in the Interview Room, I had inwardly been saying to myself, "Baba, please do not ask me what I want, because You know what I want. I want to love You and serve You for the rest of my life."

As I sat by His Holy Feet, He said so sweetly, "Baba has something for you." With that, He circled His hand again and out came a beautiful diamond ring. He indicated for me to hold out my hand for Him to put the ring on my finger, but when I held out my right hand,

He said, "No, other hand." I held out my left hand, and He placed it on my ring finger; it was a perfect fit.

That night, as I lay in my bed in the Ashram, I took off the ring and had a good look at it. To tell you the truth, the gold band felt a bit rough, and I heard myself say, "Baba this ring is a bit rough."

Then came the reply, "Yes, many rough edges, I will help smooth." Wow, Baba was going to help me smooth out my rough edges and help me become a better human being by doing so. I felt truly blessed.

After this Interview, I felt as if finally there was real meaning to my life. I felt protected and loved for who I truly am. In difficult times, I had always felt this same feeling, but now it had a name, a form, a very dear face.

When I got back from India, my workload started increasing at Jack's clinic, as well as my own clinic in London. It was therefore difficult for me to return to India as often as I would have liked. But in the spare time I could find, I would devour books written about other people's divine experiences with Sai Baba. I would often feel His presence when I was doing my healing work and felt closer and closer to Him as the months went by.

While I had not grown up with a permanent role model, I now had one. I felt so blessed and would forever express my gratitude to Him. During this time, I also had several dreams of Sai Baba, which I have recorded in a special notebook. One particular one is significant, when I dreamt that I was down by a riverbed with Sai Baba, where He dunked me in the water three times. He then blew into His hands, and a huge Om sign manifested into the air. He told me to put the sign on my front door. Since then, I have always had an Om sign on my front door.

CHAPTER 29

1997. MORE ABOUT PRINCESS DIANA

When Jack started to treat Princess Diana, he would often ask my advice on how to handle her. He had a good relationship with her, but still he sought my opinions.

There were many things that needed to be cleared in Diana. For example, she used to take sleeping pills when she traveled abroad called Halcion, which later in 1991 were taken off the market, as the risks far outweighed their benefits. Some of the side-effects were depression and anxiety. There is no doubt, when Diana first consulted Jack, that she was in turmoil and possibly in depression. When she was treated for the various components that Jack felt were disturbing Diana's nervous system, she gradually became more of her own person; stronger in her determination to become a woman in her own right. She was not a religious person as such, but she was spiritual. I personally believe, if I had spent more time with her, we could have drawn out this side of her, which would have given her more comfort and support. Diana was also a wonderful listener and would draw people out of themselves.

The essential truth lies in the inner consciousness of ourselves, not external organized actions. The critiques must be removed if a person is to be able to walk by herself. When you have something to prove, you are not free. This was Diana's weakness. She was not capable of being totally free. I think if she had lived longer and matured a bit more, she would have found freedom and peace.

June 1996. EXHIBITION IN KENSINGTON PALACE, WITH ART BY PAUL GAISFORD, THAT SARAH ORGANIZED FOR HER CHARITY, CHILDREN IN CRISIS

It was a wonderful evening, and Princess Diana was on good form. Prince Andrew came up to me and planted a red sticker on my jacket and said with a big smile, "You are sold." He always made me laugh and smile. We had a very special friendship that was founded on mutual respect.

The following year, after Diana passed away, I had a breakfast meeting in Tallahassee Florida with the owners of Findhorn Press, who were friends of mine, about another book I was wanting to publish. They told me about a Norwegian Channeler by the name of Rita Eide, who had sent them a draft of a book she had written about being channelled by Princess Diana. They asked me to vet the book and author. This I did.

I was living in Panama City Beach Florida at the time and invited Rita Eide to come and stay with me for a few days after reading the draft of her book. During her stay, I asked her to channel Diana for me. Eventually, she did, and I taped the recording. Diana came through and started off by saying "Dearest Heart," which she and Sarah, Duchess of York, used to call me and I them. Goosebumps appeared on my arms, as I felt this was promising. Diana proceeded to say that if she had known who I truly was, she would have consulted me at a deeper level. She also said that Charles and Camilla were soulmates and they were destined to be together. She seemed light and happy, indicating that she was now doing important work on the other side. She said that she often visited her beloved boys and they were aware of her visits. (This is interesting, as Prince Harry mentioned in his resent autobiography *Spare,* that he often feels his mother's presence.) Diana also said that forgiveness was the most important thing we could accomplish, to whomever we considered to have done us wrong, as this was the only way of being free.

Rita's book was published by Findhorn Press in 1999 under the title *The Celestial Voice of Diana: Her Spiritual Guidance to Finding Love.*

CHAPTER 30

1997. MY FIRST MEETING WITH DOLPHINS

After Princess Diana passed away, I found myself in a difficult place. It had really affected me, as it did Jack. In October 1997, I took my daughter, Natasha, to Panama City Beach in North West Florida to swim with the wild dolphins as a 21st birthday present for her. We stayed in the beautiful Marriott Hotel on Panama City Beach, where the most friendly wild dolphins are to be found.

The first day was spent on a boat, being guided by Dr Michel Atlas, a wild dolphin expert. Michel was a gentle, intelligent man, who showed us how to behave once the dolphins came swimming up to our boat. I shall never forget the moment I first looked into the eye of a wild dolphin. The tears just rolled down my cheeks. It seemed to last a lifetime of joy whilst I communicated with this dolphin. Even Dr Atlas was in tears as he watched my interaction with the dolphin. Afterwards, he told me that a great communication had taken place between me and the dolphin.

That night, Natasha and I fell asleep in our hotel bedroom. I can still vividly remember our room to this day. Two large double beds, one for her, one for me. I fell asleep, happy and also excited about the next day, with another promise of swimming with the wild dolphins ahead of us. At some point, I started dreaming. Then suddenly in my dream appeared the late Princess Diana. She was standing with her adopted goddaughter, who had died of cancer some years previously.

As they looked down at me, Diana spoke and said, "Leonora, do you remember my goddaughter, Leonora?"

"Yes," I said, "How could I forget? Especially when we have the same name."

Diana said, "We have come to ask you if you would care to move to Florida and work with the wild dolphins?" She continued, "So many young children are dying of cancer and other forms of illness. They will so love to come and swim with the dolphins, as dolphins are great healers."

As I was just about to answer, I woke up to my daughter shouting, "YES?", sitting up in her bed, looking around the room, then falling back on her pillow asleep.

The next morning, as we sat having breakfast on

our terrace, I asked Natasha if she'd had a dream during the night.

Taking a large piece of toast to her mouth, she casually said no, then suddenly put her toast down, looked at me and announced, "Well, yes, mum, as a matter of fact I did. I had the weirdest dream. I heard someone shouting my name, and there stood Princess Diana with a little girl, and there were all these dolphins swimming about."

Each day just got more magical, as more dolphins came up to communicate with us. We swam in the warm water and were saturated by dolphin love, as they swam around us, sometimes allowing us to play with them. It almost felt as if they knew the inner secrets of my soul, assuring me that all was well, to just relax and let life unfold itself in perfect timing.

New friendships also sprung up between Dr Atlas, as well as his son, who was helping with the boat trips, myself and Natasha. It was hard to imagine leaving this paradise. I had got very attached to some special dolphins that came and swam with us every day. Dolphins treat you immediately like an old friend. You lose all sense of time and place. Suddenly, you feel your heart opening up fully and you experience unconditional love for yourself, other human beings and nature. You are then fully living in the moment, which is the most valuable gift we can give ourselves for self-healing.

When it came time to leave, we were very tearful. Dr Atlas asked me if I would consider coming back to help him with his dolphin program and research. I said I would think about it.

As the plane took off and we were flying over Panama City, looking down on the magnificent beaches we had left behind, as well as special dolphin friends, Natasha turned to me and said, "Mum, why don't you come back and live here for a while?" I contemplated her suggestion, plus the many phone calls from Dr Atlas on my return, as well as the dream I'd had regarding Princess Diana, asking me to work with sick children and dolphins, which was a big persuasion. Thus, I started thinking about embarking on a new adventure to move to Florida.

But before I did, I decided to go to India once again to see my Beloved Guru. I gathered a group of doctors and therapists who came with me. When we arrived in Prasanthi Nilayam Ashram, we got called in for an Interview almost immediately. It was just before Sai Baba's 71st birthday on 23rd November 1997, and we had all written "Happy Birthday Baba" on a beautiful photo of a wild dolphin, which I presented to Sai Baba. He sat with it in His lap for a long time.

He then looked at me and said, "Fish?"

I said, "No, Baba, dolphin."

He smiled and said, "Yes, dolphin. Dolphins open the Heart Chakra. You go." So there I had my answer I had been looking for, even before asking Him. I wanted His approval that I was doing the right thing moving to Florida to work with the wild dolphins.

Many of the people present during this Interview had an opportunity to speak with Sai Baba about their work. Baba would give them advice on this, that and the other, sometimes reprimanding them on some aspect of their work. Finally, I picked up the courage to ask Baba about my healing work.

He looked at me tenderly, raising both His arms in benediction, and said, "I am always with you when you work." I have never felt so much love and encouragement in my life; enough to last a lifetime. During this Interview, Baba also told me, "You have understood forgiveness at the deepest level. Very happy."

Then Sai Baba looked at Michel Atlas, who had also come along on the trip, and created a beautiful ring for him. Baba said, "Very good man." As Baba's gaze fell on me, He said, "Only friends." Michel was very upset about this revelation, as he had high hopes for a relationship with me. I naturally went right off the idea and decided to follow Sai Baba's advice.

During this stay in the Ashram, I went to see Mr Chakravarti, the Sri Sathya Sai Central Trust, Secretary, who had looked after my group I had brought previously with the Duchess of York, who told me then to always come and see him when I visited the Ashram. I felt very fortunate, not having to join the long queue of people waiting to see him at his office, and was allowed to go straight into the building and announce myself to his secretaries. I would not have to wait long before I was led into Mr Chakravarti's office, sometimes whilst he was still with important people. He would then introduce me to them all as the 'Healer' and ask me to sit and absorb the conversation going on. During this particular visit, when the room had emptied and we were alone, he asked me what was on my mind. I told him that I would love an interview with Dr Safaya, who was the head of the Super Speciality Hospital, to ask him if I could sometimes work in the hospital. He picked up the phone, spoke to Dr Safaya, and an appointment was made for the next day.

I always love going to the Super Speciality Hospital in Puttaparthi, as it is like entering a sacred Temple. The story behind the legend of this hospital is nothing short of one massive miracle.

When Isaac Tigrett, founder of the Hard Rock Café, came to visit Sai Baba in 1984 to thank Him for saving his life after having crashed his car, witnessing Sai Baba lift him out of the mangled car, he became totally committed to serving Sai Baba. But it took fifteen years of continually visiting His Ashram, being ignored by Sai Baba during those years. Finally, the day came when Isaac was asked to go in for Interview. During this Interview, Sai Baba asked him what he wanted. The answer came back from Isaac, "To love You and serve You."

Isaac decided to sell the Hard Rock Café on the stock market. It sold for 108 million dollars, which is what Sai Baba had predicted.

As soon as the money was in the bank from the sale, Isaac went back to the Ashram with half the amount, for the contribution towards the building of the new Super Speciality Hospital.

Designed in three months and constructed in nine months!

This 300-bed tertiary care hospital was equipped with fourteen operating theatres, one intensive care unit, two cardiac catheterisation laboratories, five in-patient wards and a 24-hour emergency unit. It has a staff of specialists in cardiology, urology, ophthalmology, plastic surgery, orthopaedics, gastroenterology, anaesthesiology, laboratory services and medical imaging. Doctors from all over the world come to work there and give their time for free. All facilities and operations are totally free of cost to all patients.

So there I was, sitting in this magnificent hospital, about to have my meeting with Dr Safaya. He was a most interesting man to talk to. We talked about my work, but as he pointed out to me, because I did not have a medical degree, it would not be appropriate for me to come and work in the hospital; no matter how much Sai Baba appreciated my healing work, he had been told!

On the day we all left Sai Baba's Ashram, we had agreed amongst us that if we did not get another Interview, we would have a leisurely breakfast in the Western canteen and then leave for the airport. As Darshan started, Baba came into the Temple, and as He passed me, I asked Him for another Interview. He stopped, looked at me for a long time, then smiled and said, "Yes, special interview," and moved on.

My group got all excited and said, "Get up, Leonora, Baba said interview."

I said, "No, He did not say 'Go'. He means something else."

Dejected, we all went out of the Temple once Baba finished His rounds and He had stepped into the Interview Room and closed the door.

As we were sitting having breakfast, I suddenly got all hot and funny. Before I knew what was happening, I started to say in an urgent voice, "Hurry up, everyone, finish your breakfast. We have to leave NOW." Everyone looked at me as if I had gone soft in the head, making objections, as we had all agreed that we would have plenty of time to have a leisurely breakfast, then slowly gather our belongings and board the minibus we had ordered to drive us to the airport in Bangalore. I kept repeating we needed to leave *now*. Everyone decided we'd better do just that to appease me.

Within a short time, we were all seated in the minibus and heading out of the Ashram gate. Nobody said a word, just sat glaring at me with sour faces. I felt dreadful but knew that something special was about to happen. Sure enough, after we had driven up the Hight Street and turned the corner on the road, at the roundabout, our driver suddenly shouted, "Ma'am, look, Baba is in front of us."

I rushed up and sat on the spare seat next to the driver, and sure enough, there was Baba's car in front of us. There was also a jeep behind His car, with two men standing on the foot fall on either side of it. They kept beckoning us to come closer then to stop if we got too close. It was obvious that this was for us. Suddenly, Baba threw a garland out of His car window, and everyone shouted, "Stop the bus so we can pick up the garland." I said, "No, we need to follow Baba. He is probably going to visit the Super Speciality Hospital up the road."

Hardly able to breathe, we continued to follow. As we came to the hospital, Baba's car carried on. Oh wow, were we really so fortunate as to be following Baba all the way to Bangalore? But no, something much more special occurred. About 300 meters past the hospital, the jeep and Baba's car stopped. The men on the jeep jumped down and told us to get out of the bus. When we were all standing on the road, Baba's car turned around. As He slowly drove past us, He raised His arms in blessing. We watched Baba's car until we could no longer see it, tears rolling down our cheeks in gratitude for being guided out of holy Puttaparthi by our Guru. The road was mysteriously deserted, except for one car that was parked about 200 yards behind our bus.

We bordered our bus in silence. I asked everyone to sit with their own interpretation of what had just happened. Sometime later, we stopped at the Halfway Café, before arriving at Bangalore airport, to freshen up and have a cup of tea.

This was when I was approached by a couple, who came up to me asking who I was. I told them my name was Leonora. They said, "No, who are you?" I looked at them with a puzzled look on my face, wondering what they were getting at. They then proceeded to tell me that they had witnessed what had happened back by the Super Specialist Hospital, when they realized that we were following Baba's car. As soon as they tried to catch up with us, their car had stopped dead! They tried in vain to restart it, but to no avail. So they sat patiently until Baba had passed them, when their car started up again! They also told me that they had lived in Puttaparthi for twenty years and were up and down the road to Bangalore often, but they had never witnessed what had happened at our 'special interview' with the Blessings from Baba, which indicated it was just for our benefit.

Thank you, Baba, we are deeply grateful and humbled for this amazing blessing You afforded us.

My Sai Group in Soukya with Dr Mathai

CHAPTER 31

1997. A NEW LIFE BEGINS IN FLORIDA

On 19th December 1997, I departed for Florida. I sold my house and business in the UK, much to the utter dismay of Prince Andrew and Sarah, my family and my friends. Talk about taking another leap of faith!

I spent Christmas with my older sister and her husband, who live in California. Michel Atlas drove from Florida to join us. We had a wonderful time together, my sister being the best hostess ever. Michel had arrived with the first CD I had ever heard of Dana Gillespie, singing Sai Baba Devotional Songs. I found myself going into pure bliss whilst listening to this CD over and over again, my longing to go back to India, to spend time with my Divine Spiritual Master, ever present in my heart.

MY NEW YEAR CALL WITH PRINCE ANDREW

On New Year's Day, a few weeks after my arrival in America, I got a call from Prince Andrew. He started the conversation by saying, "Leonora, do you want the good news or the bad news?"

I said, "Give me the good news first."

He said, "My mother wants to meet you."

After a moment of stunned silence, I managed to say, "Wonderful, I can't wait. Now please give me the bad news."

He proceeded to say that during the family Christmas dinner, when it came time to pull the Christmas crackers, his mother's cracker had revealed a pendulum.

She'd held it up and said, "What is this?"

Andrew replied, "Mother, that is a pendulum. Let me show you how to use it."

(Before I had left for Florida, I had given Andrew and Sarah a beautiful pendulum each and taught them how to use it.)

Andrew showed his mother how to let the pendulum give a yes and a no, and soon she was dousing like a pro.

He said, "The bad news is that my mother seems to be a better dowser than Jack Temple!" We both burst into peals of laughter.

During the time I knew Prince Andrew, before my departure at the end of 1997 to set up my Dolphin Healing Centre in Northwest Florida, I can only say that he was a very quiet and often shy person, who was nothing but kindness itself. We had wonderful talks about spiritual matters, as well as other issues that were troubling him. On my last evening before my departure to Florida, he invited me to Sunninghill Park to have dinner with him. The staff had set up a table for two in the alcove of the big dining room, where we enjoyed a special dinner together, after having tucked up in bed the two princesses, who were full of questions about dolphins and when would it be possible for them to come and visit me.

After dinner we went to his study and had a long talk about God. I remember him also saying, "Leonora, why do you think I was born a Prince?" It felt a troubled, loaded question, which I could give no answer to.

Recently, I received the most beautiful letter from him, thanking me for the condolences I had sent him after his mother's passing. I had tears in my eyes when I had finished reading it. Several times since the Queen's passing, she has come into my dreams, looking worried about her beloved son. In one dream she seemed to be saying, "I know Andrew would never willingly have done anything to embarrass or hurt either me or his family, who mean everything to him."

I am dismayed at the recent events that have so drastically turned his life around. When Andrew was appointed the UK's special representative for International Trade and Investment, he thought it beneficial to associate with Jeffrey Epstein, who, at that time, was highly regarded as a prominent businessman. It seems now, that Epstein was also a master at blackmailing influential people he had made friends with. I would not be at all surprised to discover, that the infamous photo of Prince Andrew with Virginia Giuffre was set up for precisely that reason: blackmail. Like all of us, Prince Andrew has made some big mistakes, but have we not all done so? Who said he was supposed to be the perfect person, who could never make mistakes and not allowed to be forgiven? I sincerely pray that he will find peace in his soul and forgive those people who now seem to despise him.

Soon, it was time for Michel and I to say our goodbyes to my sister and her husband and head off across America to Northwest Florida. We booked into the Bell Aires Hotel, where I had stayed many times in the past, to do filming work. For some reason, I had a panic attack before going to sleep, worried about going to live in Florida. I had left so many wonderful friends behind in England, for the unknown. I was crying my heart out to God, asking if this was really what I was meant to do now, to be of best service to humanity. The answer came back loud and clear, in the form of two huge, I mean *huge* angels standing by my bed. I had NEVER seen an angel before, let alone two! Then a man appeared to arrive as well, dressed in an orange robe. The familiar Voice asked me not to be distressed, that all would be well and I would be doing a great service to many people in need of dolphin healing. That was good enough for me, and I fell asleep dreaming of dolphins.

Arriving in Panama City Beach, I booked into the Marriott Hotel, where I had stayed before. Every day I would look for a house to set up my new healing work. Finally, I decided upon a lovely big house, not far from the harbour at the Marriott Hotel, which would give me easy access to moor a boat.

The first months were spent helping Dr Michel Atlas and his partner get their business in order. Soon it became clear that their dolphin business was in financial trouble. It got so bad that Michel no longer could afford to stay in his rented house, so I allowed him to come and live in mine, with his son and their dog, which was a grumpy old thing that was apt to nip at any new person entering my home.

For my 50th birthday, I decided it would be a good idea to invite friends from all over the world to celebrate by swimming with the dolphins. Invitations went out and many replied that they would come. Jack came with my two girlfriends in tow, who had advised him to buy some suntan lotion at the airport. He used it and woke up in the morning to a dark orange face. He had bought tanning lotion instead of suntan lotion! My girlfriends and I still laugh about this funny incident.

Most of my friends booked a three-day program to swim with the dolphins, which they paid Michel's company for. Every passing month, I would inject money into his business, until finally I'd had enough, after giving tens of thousands of pounds. I still have the IOUs he insisted on writing, but I have never seen a dollar back from him. I eventually had to ask Michel to leave my house, also informing him that I could sadly no longer support him, his son, or his business.

CHAPTER 32

1998. I SET UP MY OWN DOLPHIN HEALING CENTRE

In no time, I was up and running my own dolphin healing business. I had an article published in Dr Horace Dobbs' 'Dolphin Magazine'. Soon people came from all over the world to stay in my home for a week's adventure and healing with the wild dolphins.

It was a frantically busy time for me. I used to personally pick up the visitors at the airport and take them back to my home, where they had beautiful en-suit accommodation. I used to teach them how to snorkel in my pool and how to behave when coming across a wild dolphin in the ocean. We had magical times with the special ambassador dolphins that used to come up to my boat every day. There they would do their *'zona scanning'*, when healing would take place. Swimming in the warm ocean waters with the wild dolphins off the coast of Panama City Beach and Shell

Island close by was truly an experience that was out of this world. Many families with sick children came to stay with me, experiencing healing.

One such family was Angie Buxton King and her son Sam, whom Jack Temple and I had treated back in England when he was diagnosed with leukaemia. Sam was very ill when he arrived with his mother, father and brother. The doctors had devised a special Hickman line for him so he could go in the water to swim with the dolphins. Angie has written a book, *The NHS Healer,* about her son's illness and his visit to Florida swimming with the wild dolphins. After a wonderful happy week in my home and beautiful encounters with the dolphins, they all left with no doubt that it had been a perfect family holiday.

Soon after they arrived home, Sam passed to spirit. I wonder if the dolphins had given him the courage to do so? Dear sweet gentle spirit Sam, we love you and miss you so much, but know you are happy where you are now, with no pain.

Angie and her husband, Graham, have set up a charity in memory of Sam called The Sam Buxton Sunflower Healing Trust. It's aim is to provide integrated care for cancer patients in the UK. Angie is now also the Head of Complementary Therapies and Foundation for Integrated Health (FIH). After all these years, Angie is still a dear friend and is in fact a trustee of my Charity, Sai Grace Trust CIO. Recently, her husband died. I was honoured to conduct his funeral.

The other day, as Angie and I were walking along the beach in Aldeburgh, which we do periodically, she told me of the dream she'd had before arriving in Florida with Sam, which she had never told me before. She had dreamt of Princess Diana and her goddaughter, Leonora, surrounded by dolphins!

Another family came with a five-year-old child who had Down's Syndrome and had not yet learnt to speak. The first day when we went out on my boat, we were soon surrounded by dolphins. The child and I sat on a special platform on my boat, where you could sit with your feet in the water. One particular dolphin started to show great interest in us. It swam round and round, then stood still in the water and started 'scanning' the child. Suddenly, the child turned to her father and said, "Daddy, Dolphin." From that moment on, the child made great strides in her development. To this day, I am in touch with her. She calls me her dolphin teacher. She has gone to university and is making a good life for herself.

CHAPTER 33

1998. ENTER MY AMERICAN HUSBAND - TO BE OR NOT TO BE!

After living in Florida for a while, I was introduced by mutual friends to an American lobbyist. He used to come to Panama City to visit his mother most weekends. He got to hear about my experiences with Sai Baba.

One day, I got a call from him asking if he could come and talk to me about my meetings with Sai Baba. I told him that I was a deep admirer of Sai Baba, having had several interviews with Him, and it would be my pleasure to tell him about my experiences. This man was also greatly impressed with Sai Baba, as he had recently been to India to meet Him. During his time in the Temple, Sai Baba had come up to him and said, "No more smoking, no more meat and no more alcohol." But he had not been given an interview, which he was longing for. When he got back to his home, he stopped smoking, eating meat and drinking alcohol, all in one hit.

Slowly, a sweet friendship sprung up between Don and myself. I even permitted myself to *maybe* fall in love with him, after a long time of having no boyfriend in my life. We both had such love for Sai Baba and spent many happy hours reading to each other from books written about our Spiritual Teacher.

Every weekend, Don would come and stay in my house and sometimes came out to help me with my Dolphin Swims. We would go for lovely long walks at night along the magnificent beaches on Panama City Beach, sometimes eating at the restaurants there, looking at the setting sun. Very romantic and charming was this time in my life.

After a few months, we decided to go to India and stay in Sai Baba's Ashram. We did not get a converted Interview when we went there, but we had a special time anyway. I had interviews with Sai Baba most times I had been in the past and I had a deep suspicion that Don was very disappointed that we had not been given one.

But one interesting thing did happen while we were there. First of all, it was not allowed for unmarried people to share a room, but when we handed our passports in at the accommodation office, they gave us just one key. This indicated to us that Sai Baba did not mind us sharing a room. In fact, this was doubly made clear to us when we went down to the accommodation office the next day and heard the man sitting at the booking window saying to a couple in front of us, "No, I cannot give you a single room, as it is not permissible for non-married couples to share a room."

On one occasion, while we were in the Ashram, we had a discussion with some fellow Americans we had met about whether, when we have dreams of Sai Baba, it really is Him coming into our dreams. That night when I was getting ready for bed, I was in the bathroom and continued the conversation with Baba in my head about what we had talked about earlier that day, whether it is truly Him coming into our dreams. I heard Sai Baba saying, that if the dream is so strong and it is unforgettable in details, then it is definitely Him coming into our dreams, usually with a message. I was satisfied with this answer and told myself I would tell Don when I was finished brushing my teeth.

As I came out of the bathroom, I saw Don sitting on his bed with his eyes on stalks and mouth wide open. I went over to him, asking him if he was alright. He said, "Who was in the bathroom with you?" I said, "What are you talking about?" He proceeded to tell me that he had definitely heard me talking to a male voice in the bathroom. I then asked him what he had heard me say. To my astonishment, he proceeded to relate word-for-word the conversation I'd had in my head with Sai Baba in the bathroom. We both agreed that what Baba had demonstrated through Don witnessing this conversation was nothing but astounding and must be the truth. So now when I dream of Sai Baba, I know for sure it is Him who comes into my dreams with a message. More of that later.

Slowly, I started falling in love with Don, who was as devoted to Sai Baba as I was. I think this was the aspect I loved the most about him. I met his family, and they liked me, as I liked them in return. But something was not quite right. I do not think it would be prudent for me to write too much about my experiences with Don's sometimes deep depressions, but it was an uphill climb every time. It became clear to me that Don was not happy within himself. Therefore, it became a struggle to keep him happy while trying not to become resentful that he had little understanding about how stressful it was for me living in America as an alien, only allowed to stay for three months at a time, then having to come back, never knowing if I would be rejected for re-entry.

When I told Don I had a buyer for my home and wanted to return to England, he asked me to marry him. What was it Sai Baba had said all those years ago? "Sometimes a little mad?" Well, this was another of those mad decisions in my life that I could have spent a bit more time thinking about and then coming to the right decision. Although I loved this man, I knew something was not right. He insisted that after meditating he had inwardly been told to marry me. I accepted.

One month later, we got married at a friend's beautiful house in Georgia. An hour before the ceremony, Don slapped a pre-nuptial on me, which basically said that I had no claim whatsoever to a penny of his estate if we ever divorced. This was a bit of a shock to me, as we had not discussed the matter before the wedding. It was not a problem for me, as I had my own money and could look after myself, as I had done for the past 33 years. It was the way it was done that felt out of order. Even his best man looked at him in surprise and said I should have been consulted beforehand.

Shortly after the wedding, we flew to India to have a blessing of our marriage from Sai Baba. It was wonderful to be back in the home of my Beloved Guru, where I always felt truly welcomed. At the first Darshan, Baba came up to me, looked at me, and said, "Very happy, very happy." This to me meant that Sai

Baba had approved of our marriage. But my husband wanted an Interview, so I told him to take our Wedding Service Sheet and give it to Baba. The following morning, Baba come to where my husband was sitting, took the Wedding Sheet and blessed it in between His hands three times and said, "Very happy, very happy, very happy."

When I got back to our room, I saw a half-pleased look on my husband's face. He was happy but still insisted he wanted an Interview with Baba. I felt exasperated, knowing that this might not be possible. We left India with no Interview. I had a raging fever by now, as I could feel the disappointment raging inside my husband. All the way back to Florida, he hardly spoke a word to me.

On our return to Florida, the plan was to spend a few days in my house before my husband had to go back to his work in Tallahassee. We arrived home, and I had to go to bed with a chest infection. That night, we lay in bed in silence. I reached across and asked what the matter was. He said he was disappointed that our marriage had not been properly blessed! I reminded him that in fact Baba had blessed our Wedding Service Sheet. But apparently that was not good enough for Don.

Then I heard myself say in a tired voice: "Do you want a divorce?"

To my utter shock, he got out of bed, took off his wedding ring, handed it to me and said, "Yes, that would be nice." With those words ringing in my ears, he left the house.

Eleventh step towards FORGIVENESS.

Over a week went by before I managed to make contact with my husband. He said he wanted some time on his own and would contact me shortly. A further week went by and still no word. By now, I felt utterly despondent. I was trying to recover from my brush with pneumonia and the shock of him leaving me. I consulted a lawyer but was advised I could do nothing, as we had only been married for 40 days and 40 nights! Later, I discovered that the lawyer I had consulted was a good friend of my husband!

The weeks that followed were very painful indeed. I suffered all sorts of attacks on myself, wondering what I could have done to avoid this disaster. But this was also a brilliant time for me to start doing some more serious inner work. I went into deep meditation every day and felt closer to my Spiritual Master than ever before. Often, I would get answers from my crying questions. One day, I was lying on my bed; the French doors leading out onto the terrace were open and the curtains were blowing gently in the breeze. I was in a state of contemplation, when suddenly, in answer to a question, I heard my Guru's voice saying, "Die mind, die mind, die mind", nine times in total. I fell into a space where there was only peace. Another time I heard a continuous "Aum" coming from outside the terrace door. It just went on and on, lulling me into a state of bliss. Then I heard my Guru's voice say, **"Bangaru, you are doing well. You are again learning forgiveness at the deepest level. Learn to accept that your love for your husband is greater than your need of him."** This utter state of bliss lasted for days. I felt as if my pain was literally beginning to melt away.

CHAPTER 34

1999. BACK TO INDIA FOR ANSWERS

Having lost the buyer for my home, when I had first wanted to go back to UK, I now found it impossible to find another buyer as the housing market had slowed down. So I decided to rent it out for five months before my next dolphin season would begin.

After over a month of little communication with my husband, I decided to go back to India to spend some time with Sai Baba. Also to see if I could get the opportunity of asking Him why, when He had blessed our Wedding Service Sheet, it had ended after only 40 days and 40 nights! A few days after my arrival and sitting in my usual place of first line in the Ashram Temple, Sai Baba came up to me. He stood there smiling. I asked Him if I could have an Interview. He just continued smiling. Then He created some Vibhuti for me and said in His sweet, low voice, "Karmic marriage, very happy. Keep working at forgiveness."

No Interview was granted during my stay, so over time, I had to work it out for myself. I think it must go something like this: sometimes, we have to have a certain experience to release some karma from the past. Could I have behaved the same way in a past life, as my husband had behaved towards me in this lifetime? Could it be that to release the Karma, I had to experience the same sort of treatment? Yes, I think so. It makes sense. Otherwise, it makes no sense whatsoever. This then gave me the opportunity to continue working on FORGIVENESS at an ever-deeper level.

But what does make sense is that in re-reading my diary entries during this time, I note how Baba was continuously coming into my dreams almost every night, guiding me, encouraging me and simply letting me know He was there for me. This sustained me and helped me get through a most difficult time.

It came to me that you have to break to heal. When it comes to forgiveness, you have to understand it by first feeling the hurt, the sorrow, the anger, the despair of violated boundaries before it can pass into love. So I worked hard at validating the parts of me that felt bruised, abused and abandoned, the shattered reality that I might have made an almighty mistake in not listening to my intuition. I tried to understand the trap I had landed myself in, then slowly drenched it in forgiveness. I had to open my heart to myself, to understand the heart of the one who had hurt me. Slowly, forgiveness dropped into the depths of my soul, finding the wholeness that was never taken from me, the eternal being that I am. It took time and effort, but I was in the best place, getting the support from my loving Guru, who was ever looking after my every emotional needs by His loving presence and sweet smiles.

After our marriage, and when we had come to the Ashram for our honeymoon to seek Baba's blessings, my husband and I had bought an apartment, just outside the Ashram, which we shared the costs of. It needed decorating, as it had only just been built. I was working very hard on getting the apartment in perfect order, when I got a surprise call from my husband to say that he and his brother were coming for a visit over the Christmas period. I had no objections to this and enjoyed getting the apartment ready for their arrival. I shall never forget my husband's face when he walked in the door. He was absolutely delighted with the results, and yes, the apartment did look amazing.

It was strange how he thought that we could just fall into a husband and wife relationship again after not seeing each other for four months and his inexplainable behaviour. I was still unsettled from his extraordinary display of no interest in being married to me, to suddenly being all over me like a hot rash. Although I thought I was still in love with him, I felt he had to prove himself first. Then the second day, he got a severe stomach bug and had to go into the little private clinic next to our apartment. I tenderly looked after him during this time, when he was on a drip and feeling very poorly.

When Don and his brother arrived, I had insisted Don take the spare bedroom, while his brother slept in the sitting room on the sofa bed. The day after Don was admitted into the clinic, I had to look through his suitcase, which he had not unpacked, to find some clean clothes for him. What did I find there? DIVORCE PAPERS! When I confronted Don as to why he had been so underhanded after pretending he wanted us to get back together again, he just shrugged and said he had brought them in case I wanted a divorce! Little did I know at the time that he had started dating his accountant and she was gunning for marriage. Sounds familiar? Well, it must be my karma to always fall for these handsome, deceitful men. For some reason, I refused to sign the divorce papers. I kept asking Baba if I should sign, but I got the indication that I had to wait.

After my so-called husband left, I signed up to become a PEP therapist, which is a program designed to help coordinate the left and right hemisphere of the brain. This kept me occupied for a few months before my return to Florida in April, ready for my next dolphin season. When I got back to Florida, I had a happy summer, with people arriving from all over the world to spend time in my home and swimming with the wild dolphins. The PEP program proved extremely useful for treating the autistic children who came as well. One family came with two adorable children who were both autistic. I learnt so much from them, and we had special times together.

On the day of our first wedding anniversary on 20th July, I faxed my husband with the following words: "On this our first anniversary, I got to thinking what I could give you to make you happy. I know that if I sign the divorce papers, it will make you happy, so let's go for it."

I got a phone call back almost immediately.

"Do you mean that?" said my husband.

"Yes, I do," I said.

"What do you want?" was the reply.

"Nothing," I said. "Just the money I put into our apartment in India."

"Are you sure?" said my husband.

"Yes," I said.

A week later, he came down to my house with the divorce papers. I was a bit emotional to say the least.

I asked if we could sign them in my prayer room in front of Sai Baba's picture. We signed the papers, and strangely, we both cried. There was still a sadness inside me, but I was learning the art of forgiveness, as my love for him *had* succeeded my need for him.

I found the following letter I wrote to him shortly after this meeting:

"Our time together has started to change, and we are changing with it. Given all this change, when it comes to our relationship, we have gone about as far as we can go. We have got from each other as we can reasonably expect. I understand that our relationship was not perfect but a fleeting moment in time. Without each other, we can better come into our wholeness, as our souls are no longer willing to engage in struggle. They want something better, something easier. We are longing to become aware that we survive better as spiritual beings, if the relationship in personality is not conducive. Our souls are struggling to insist that we come into full maturity, to express the full awareness of ourselves. This is best done in either a relationship that has nothing but goodness for the other person and not allowing self-indulgence to come in the way. There is a magical mantra for all couples: "What can I bring to this relationship, rather than what can I

take from it." There is a remembrance, that what needs to be nurtured every time we fall in love, each time we trust or surrender or forgive, each time we blossom with compassion, that love for a companion on this holy journey we are traveling can and must only be the best for the two people concerned.

I will always wish you well but will not let our shared memories, however fleeting, define me. I state in all sincerity that I forgive you, including myself, and I want to release the past with love and acceptance."

Me in our apartment overlooking Sai Baba's ashram in Puttaparthi

I decided that the best thing for me to do was to go back to England, which is what I had wanted to do in the first place, before Don had asked me to marry him. My mother was aging and needed some support. I also wanted to be closer to my daughter. I put my house on the market again. When I did finally manage to find another buyer, I had to reduce the original price considerably from when I had first put it on the market, hence a big loss for me money-wise. Thank you, Don!

But before I leave the story of Florida behind, I want to tell you an amazing incident that happened as I was packing up my home to move back to UK. I was in the garage, which had a long pull-down ladder up into the loft space. I pulled it down to have a look to see if I had left anything up there that needed packing. As I started my descent, my foot slipped, and I fell about 15 feet onto the hard concrete floor. As I did so, I felt as if I had landed on a soft mattress. I had the instant thought that something or someone had saved me, and with that my left arm landed on the concrete. I lay there feeling a lot of pain. I managed to call a girlfriend, who came and took me to the hospital, where it was announced that I had broken my arm in a couple of places. I was told I would need an operation under anaesthetic and had to stay overnight. I told the doctor this was not possible, as I had to be at the airport the next morning to pick up a family who were coming to stay in my house for a week to swim with the dolphins, therefore I couldn't be all groggy after an anaesthetic. I told them they had to do the operation without it.

After much discussion, they decided they would try and go ahead to reset it without an anaesthetic, but if I was in too much pain, they would stop. I told them not to worry, I would be fine, because I would go into meditation and ask my Guru for help.

By now there were about three doctors and several nurses around me. I started chanting the Gayatri Mantra and the Sai Gayatri. I asked Sai Baba to be with me. I looked into the right corner of the operating room and saw Baba standing there, smiling. I then looked into the left corner and again saw Baba standing there smiling. I looked behind me and again saw Him standing and smiling. I knew I was going to be fine. The next thing, I heard one of the doctors saying, "It is over, you can come back now." I looked down at my arm, and it was fully covered by plaster of Paris. I had felt no pain whatsoever! The doctors and nurses were amazed and kept asking me what I had been chanting and to 'Whom'.

That night as I went to bed, I thanked my Baba, for not only saving me from deadly injuries as I fell, but also for being with me during the setting of my broken arm, allowing me to feel no pain.

My last day with my wild dolphin 1999

Dolphin saying goodbye

CHAPTER 35

2000. I MOVE BACK TO ENGLAND

In 2000, I was once again back in England, having the daunting task of finding a home for myself. I had lost a lot of money whilst in Florida, from the house sale, from lack of income, from my dealings with Dr Atlas and Don. House prices in England had soared since I had owned a house there before leaving for Florida, so finding a suitable home was not easy. My last house had been in Ascot and before that Kensington in London, but there was no way I could afford to live in either place now.

During this time of searching, I lived for a while in Jack Temple's house, who was overjoyed to have me around again. He had missed me greatly and had sent me faxes several times a week whilst I was in Florida, telling me about his daily activities. I still have these faxes, which one day will make a fascinating book in themselves.

This was also the time I became a Reiki Master, which has been a wonderful blessing, as I have taught many sweet souls Reiki healing over the years. My Reiki Master Initiation took place in Scotland, conducted by a friend who had a Healing Centre overlooking Lock Tay. The day of the Initiation arrived. We walked up the hill to the castle just outside Fortingall and sat on a big stone in a riverbed. It was raining cats and dogs, but as soon as the Initiation started, the sky parted and the sun shone from a blue patch, directly down on us. It was a surreal experience but one I felt was blessed by the Higher Beings I had encountered when I'd had my first Reiki treatment in London in 1994.

One of the last couples who had come to my Retreat Centre in Florida to swim with the dolphins was a couple from Suffolk, by the name of Jackie and David Gillett. They had heard about me from Dr Horace Dobbs and were keen to come and have the wild dolphin experience. They arrived looking bedraggled and tired. They were both energy healers in the highest degree. We spent a beautiful week together, having magical experiences with my special dolphins. They insisted that when I got back to England, I should come and visit them. They were just about to start a Healing Centre and wanted to use me as a consultant.

BEAUTIFUL SUFFOLK CALLS

I duly arrived in Suffolk one fine day in January 2000 and spent a wonderful weekend with this special couple. They were so keen on me coming to live near them that they took me to a local estate agent to look at some properties for sale. As we walked into the estate agent, a lady was pinning photos up on a board of a house for sale. It was just what I was looking for and in my price range, so we all went to take a look at it. Three months later, I moved into a 500-year-old property, set in 3 acres of land. It needed a lot doing to it, with the stable block being ideal for conversion into accommodation for special needs people.

Shortly after I moved into my new home, my recent ex-husband and his brother came for a visit. We spent a few days together. It was interesting to see him again, but by now I was happy to be forging on with my life, without complications from anyone!

Dr Horace Dobbs was very keen for me to build the first dolphin-simulated pool in the grounds of my new home, so put me in touch with a man called Trevor. He turned out to be one of those gems the world has forgotten. We spent happy hours designing the dolphin pool, but it never managed to get off the ground because of building regulations. Instead, he helped me convert the stable block and taught me much about the land. It was hard work as we mostly did all the work ourselves. I am grateful for the good friendship and for his invaluable help.

One day, as I was mowing the huge lawns with a small lawnmower, I remember saying to Sai Baba in my exhaustion, "Dearest Baba, I need a new, more functional lawnmower, but it is an expense I don't want to have as I also need a little holiday to have a bit of a break. But it will have to be one or the other." Literally one hour later, the phone rang, and it was a lady from my bank saying that I had won a luxury holiday for two to Mauritius, all expenses paid. I could not believe the grace my dear Baba had organized for me. I took my eldest sister along, and we had a fabulous time. When I got back, I bought a sit-on lawnmower and life became a lot easier!

This was also when my first gorgeous grandson, Sam, was born. I would go to France to spend a few days with my daughter, as well as all of them coming for Christmas that first year. I was overjoyed. Two years later, my beautiful granddaughter was born. Life was good.

The next few years saw me very busy setting up my new Spiritual Healing Centre. Many people came for retreats and healing. I had a useful clinic over the stable block, where people enjoyed coming for treatments. My work really started to improve now, possibly because I was just concentrating on that. This was also when I started compiling information for a 'Good Life Good Death' workshop, which I would hold many of in the future.

It seemed a lot of rape victims came to see me for counselling. Over the years, I have helped many women who have been raped, either when they were young or as grownups. It is terribly sad to see the dead look in their eyes when they come for the first time. When I think they are ready, I pose an interesting question to them, which in most incidences has been enormously helpful for their recovery. It goes like this: "Could you consider the possibility that in a past life you may have raped this person who has raped you in this life and it was now necessary for you to feel what that experience felt like?" It is a very controversial question I pose, but somehow it suddenly lights a lamp in their eyes, and after a pause, they smile and say, "Yes, I think I can buy that, as otherwise how does it make sense?" So it seems that if we can put some understanding around a dramatic incident, it lightens the burden.

I also started to hold Sai Baba Bhajan meetings in my new home and Spiritual Healing Centre. It was wonderful to discover several Sai devotes living within a 30-mile radius. In no time, I had dozens of people attending my Sunday gatherings.

We used to all attend the Sai Baba Organization retreats each summer. One particular one I remember was held in North Wales, where Anil Kumar, Sai Baba's interpreter, was the guest speaker. He had brought a friend of his along, who had not registered to attend the Sai Organization event, therefore was not allowed to join everyone in the auditorium. Anil Kumar was furious and decided that he too would now no longer attend.

This put the Sai Organisation into a predicament. So it was that they asked me if I would stand in for Anil Kumar, who was due to speak after lunch. At short notice, I had to gather my thoughts, then decided to hand my talk over to Sai Baba and prayed He would guide me, as well as speak through me. After about 45 minutes of talking, I suddenly saw Anil Kumar and his friend come sit in the front of the auditorium. That made everyone happy, including me, who had done my duty, to the delight of the audience.

Jack Temple used to come every three months to hold a clinic at my Healing Centre. He so enjoyed these long weekends, telling me about his latest clients and also his latest lady love! We spent endless hours talking whilst walking along the seafront in Southwold or Aldeburgh. Sometimes, I would drive down to Surrey to his clinic to treat some of his clients and also Jack himself. I would spend time at his clinic and then go back to his house to cook him dinner, which he greatly appreciated. Evenings would also be spent tidying up his cupboards and cleaning his fridge!

It was during this time that I met Michael Crawford through his daughter, who lived next door to Jack's house. After we met, he used to call me most evenings and we started a gentle friendship. He came to visit me in Suffolk, and we enjoyed many cosy hours together. One day, he announced that an old girlfriend of his had developed cancer. He wanted to bring her to my Healing Centre for me to treat her, which I duly did. Michael wanted to stay with her in the self-contained cottage on my property, rather than in the main house. So before our relationship took off, I broke it off! But we remained friends, which was nice, as he is a special person to know. Who could not fall in love with Michael singing The Phantom of the Opera?

In January 2004, Jack came to stay with me for a couple of days in Suffolk before he set off for a weekend workshop he was conducting in Sussex. He seemed not his usual self after a bad cold. I was concerned for him and told him not to go to the workshop. But he insisted and set off at 5am from his house. He decided to drive back to his house that same night, but half way home, he had a bad car accident. He called me on the phone late at night and told me what had happened, but assured me he was all right. I asked him why he had not gone to the hospital for a check-up, but he had declined the ambulance men, saying he was fine, taking a taxi home instead.

The next day, I called him to see how he was. He answered the phone by his bedside, but I could hardly understand what he was saying. I called his son, who lived next door, to ask him to take a look at his father, to see if he was all right. When I called half an hour later, I was told he was fine. The next day, I called again, but Jack sounded even more incoherent. I decided to get in my car and drive down to see him. When I arrived, I was shocked to see the condition of my dear friend. There was no doubt in my mind that he must have had a stroke. I urged his son to take his father to hospital. He said he would think about it. That night, I spent hours by Jack's bedside, giving him healing through his feet. He said he felt so much better. I took a photograph of him as he lay sleeping in his bed. This was to be the last picture I ever took of Jack.

The following day, Jack's son decided it was best for him go into hospital for assessment, but no one was allowed to know where he had been taken. Fortunately, some friends of mine found the ambulance crew who had taken Jack to the hospital, so we all went to see him the next day. It was very evident from Jack's family that we were not welcome. From then on, I had to be smuggled into the hospital to see my dear friend. I used to call him at night when I was unable to come and visit (long drive from Suffolk to Surrey.) The last conversation I had with Jack was through one of the nurses on the ward, who told me that Jack was saying, "Tell her she is a great healer and she is welcome in my home any time." I think he wanted me to stay in his house so I could be closer to him.

The next time I visited Jack, he was unable to speak, and it was evident that he was dying. It was so sad to see this great man slipping away. He had wanted to live until way past 100.

I was attending a big meeting in London when I got the call from mutual friends that Jack only had a short time left to live. I dashed down to Surrey and managed to see my dear friend before he left his body. I leant over him and said, "Jack, it's me. Don't forget to wait for me wherever you end up. I am counting on you for that. Also, dear Jack, don't forget you are not the body but eternal. Soon you will be in your real home." I then gave him the other half of the pendulum he had made for us both, each half set with an emerald in a silver setting on a silver chain. As I gave it to Jack, I asked him to bless it. He took it and held it for a long time, all the while smiling, his eyes closed, which had not been open for days. He bounced it up and down in his one good hand and then indicated for me to take it, with his blessing. This is the pendulum I now use for my own patients, to spin their chakras into unison, before I start my treatments. I feel Jack there helping me and smiling down, excited beyond measure to know that the work I am doing is truly blessed. In the early hours of that morning, Jack passed away. He was a great healer, way beyond his time. He is greatly missed.

At this very moment, as I am writing about Jack, I have suddenly remembered how I encouraged him to write his own story. On one of our travels abroad, he started to use a small Dictaphone I had given him to dictate his extraordinary life story. Later, it was written and called *The Healer*. The second book was called *Medicine Man.* I specifically asked Jack not to mention me in his books by name, because it was during that time one of his daughters was pursuing me relentlessly because of her jealousy of me. So he just referred to me as his colleague, but wrote instead beautiful inscriptions on the copies of his books he gave me. One inscription read, "To my very very close friend, much love, Jack." The other inscription read, "Leonora, my dearest spiritual colleague and friend." My friends, Thierry and Karin Bogliolo, owners of Findhorn Press, published his books.

CHAPTER 36

2003. MY CALLING TO BECOME AN INTER-FAITH MINISTER

In 2003, I got the calling to become an Inter-Faith Minister. I flew back to India to spend some time in Sai Baba's Ashram. It was confirmed by Sai Baba that this would be a perfect outcome for me. So I signed up for a two-year course at the Interfaith Seminary in London. The first year was extremely interesting. I was kept very busy, also running my Healing Centre in Suffolk, as well as looking after my aging mother, whom I had sole responsibility for. She was living in a lovely care home in Kent, but it was a long journey for me every other week to spend a few days with her. In the end, I decided to combine my monthly Inter-Faith studies in London with looking after my mother.

Coming back at night from the Seminary and having to deal with my mother was not an easy time. She was becoming increasing difficult as her health deteriorated. But softness started to appear as well. Even though she was angry at God (I never understand why people get angry at God for their own mistakes), it felt as if some healing was taking place between herself and her Maker. She even started to make some nice comments about my Spiritual Master Sai Baba, instead of hurtful, spiteful ones. I shall never forget the last time I spent with her. She was lying on her bed while I was massaging her hand. She touched the diamond ring Sai Baba had materialized for me in 1997 and said, "It is a special ring, darling. Do take care of it."

This was a complete turnaround from when I had first shown it to her. Then she had said in a hurtful voice, "That's not a diamond."

I had immediately replied, "I don't care if it is a diamond or not. The mere fact that Sai Baba gave it to me is good enough."

We would also spend time talking about various aspects of 'Faith'. It was evident that before she was pierced by life's sharp edges, she'd had a loving relationship with God. She pulled out many of her quotations she had gathered in her younger days, getting great satisfaction in hearing me read them to her again after all those intervening years.

I would urge anyone who has an aging or terminally ill parent to spend time with them, to help them heal their soul and make peace before leaving their body. The last few years I spent with my mother before she died were so rewarding that I would not have missed them for anything.

Months before my mother's passing, she would call me and say,

"Darling, I think my time is up."

I would dash down to see her, but after my visit, she would rally around again. She was always talking about wanting to die in those last months she was alive. She even once, with some humour, said to me, "I have asked God, if He can't find space for me upstairs, maybe He could find some space downstairs."

Then came the day when I had my dearest friend and amazing healer, Kaya Günata, staying with me for his annual retreat at my Healing Centre. The phone rang, and it was my mother saying that she was sure she was slipping and wanted to say she loved me in case I did not get to her in time. I said, "Mama, just relax and take a little nap on your bed, I will be with you as soon as I have taken Kaya to the train station for his journey back to London."

When I got off the phone, Kaya sat me down and said, "Now listen, Leonora. Your mother needs to go, but every time you show up, she regains some strength because of your love and healing, but her soul is longing to go home. Let her go. By not going down this time, you will allow her this blessing."

It was really hard for me to follow his advice. I deeply respected the wisdom of this great man, so after depositing him at the train station, instead of driving down to my mother's, I went back home.

I went straight into my prayer room and started praying to Sai Baba to look after her and be with her if her time was up. Sai Baba had assured all of His devotees that He would look after their family members, even if they did not believe in Him. Before Kaya had left, he had given me a chart of the spine with all the nerve endings showing and their relations to every organ in the body. I placed a photo of my mother on the spine chart, then started swinging Jack Temple's pendulum, rotating it from the bottom of the spine chart up to the crown chakra, imagining it was my mother's body I was working on.

I kept repeating the words, "Mama, it is alright to leave now. You will be looked after. Don't forget to exit from the crown. Go to the Light, Mama. You are safe and I love you." All the wrong doings my mother had done towards me melted away in those moments. I felt a great peace descending on me and in me. This was a significant moment, when I realised the truth of truly going BEYOND FORGIVENESS. Shortly after, I got a call from her nursing home to say that she had been found peacefully sleeping on her bed, cuddling the teddy bear I had given her for comfort some time ago. There was no doubt in my mind that Sai Baba had heard my prayers for my mother to have a peaceful passing. I am truly grateful, my Beloved Sai.

The week my mother died was when I had to go for my first-year retreat at my Seminary. It was very fortuitous, as our founder and spiritual director, Miranda Holden, was able to spend some time with me. I expressed a wish to conduct my mother's funeral, which she and others felt was very brave of me.

Miranda was also of great support, when I told her that when I had phoned my younger half-sister with the news of our mother's passing, my sister had poured a ton of abuse at me for absolutely no apparent reason. Maybe it was her guilt that kicked in after having declined to be of any help or support in looking after our mother. I simply don't know. But on reflection, it could also be a subconscious loathing of me, as I had wonderful years with her father, who loved me dearly. She had not had that opportunity, as my mother had divorced him when she was only three years old. All I know is that I love my younger sister and have shown her that love many times in my life, but there you go. I still wonder what hurts her so badly that she felt the need to hurt me, in order to cover that hurt in herself. Maybe one day when she works it out, she will let me know. As Sai Baba so often points out, "Do not attach yourself to anybody or anything. It will only set you up for pain, sorrow and disappointment." So now I love my younger sister from a distance and hold her well-being in my prayers.

The day of my mother's funeral arrived. I felt very calm. I had spent hours writing the service, having also included several of her favourite songs, sung by her favourite person Michael Crawford. Michael had been so sweet to her and had spoken to her on the phone a couple of times, which made her very happy. One of the people who came to the funeral was my dear friend Jackie, who was the lady who had come to swim with the dolphins with her partner, David, for whom I had helped set up their Healing Centre in Suffolk. After the service, she came up to me and said, "Leonora, if I should die before you, please would you conduct my funeral for me? That was the most beautiful service I have ever witnessed."

Two days later, my phone rang, and it was a friend with the news that Jackie and David Gillett had been in a car crash and they were both dead. I was absolutely stunned. My two dear friends gone just like that. Even to this day they are greatly missed.

Unfortunately, I was not allowed to conduct Jackie's funeral, as her family wanted a traditional Jewish one, which I went to but was not impressed with. In contrast, David's funeral in Suffolk was a most dignified one, held in our local Quaker church, where I read a poem for my special friend.

Three dear friends departed, plus my mother, all in the space of six months. I was reeling. Shortly thereafter, I decided to put my house on the market, so I could concentrate on my last year at the Inter-Faith Seminary. I quickly found a buyer and sold well. With the proceeds of some of the money, I bought my daughter a lovely four-bedroom house in France, where she, her husband and my three precious grandchildren could live in comfort. They had no prospect of buying their own house, so I felt it my duty to help them get settled.

Some years later, this has been thrown back in my face, with insults and hurtful behaviour, but as I say to myself, I would not have given up the opportunity of buying that house for them for anything in the world. It feels like the best thing I ever did. My daughter has been one of my great teachers, teaching me to live attachment free, but still able to love at the deepest level. Now I enjoy precious memories that were lived in the past with her and my beautiful grandchildren.

I also manage to dive ever deeper into going BEYOND FORGIVENESS.

After the sale of my property, I went travelling around England. My car became my home, as I went from place to place. My first stop was Scotland to stay with my girlfriend, who had initiated me into a Reiki Master. She had bought 140 acres overlooking Loch Tay to start a mini Findhorn and Sai Baba Centre. It was hard work to help her get the place into some form of shape, but I worked like a beaver, as well as writing all the written work that had to be done every month for the Seminary. Whilst I was there, I fell in love with Scotland again, especially the energy around Glen Lyon and Loch Tay. Three times I bid for separate houses there; three times they fell through. That was my message; I was not to settle in Scotland, so off I went again, this time to London, where I stayed with friends in Gidia Park.

This was a really difficult time for me, as at the best of times, I do not like to stay with anyone. But my friends were wonderful, and I hope it was equally good for them to have me stay. It was increasingly difficult to find a home, prices were rising at a rapid rate, and trying to decide where to buy was proving a headache. Having bought my daughter her house, my finance had dwindled a bit!

I was enjoying the last year at my Seminary, finding the discipline of studying rewarding. It was holy fascinating to visit all the various temples of the major religions, as well as all the reading we had to get through. One visit that stood out was a visit to a Gurdwara, which is the Temple for the Sikh religion. A group of my Inter-Faith colleagues and I were invited to go to a Gurdwara by a Sikh friend of mine, where we witnessed a most precious incident. The Sikhs have a holy book called the Guru Granth Sahib. This holy book is brought out every morning into the Temple and put to bed each night with great fanfare, while they chant Waheguru, which means, 'The goal is to reach God'. When the time came to put the Granth Sahib to bed, we were invited to follow it being taken up the stairs to the holy bedroom. There we were witness to the holy book being laid to rest in a small double bed with lace bedclothes. My Sikh friend was amazed, as this was such a rare opportunity that even he himself had not been witness to.

Every month I had to have a paper ready to hand in for my course. I was in my element. My understanding and relationship with God was deepening, as was my determination to find a suitable place to set up another Spiritual Healing Centre.

A very interesting event occurred during the

Seminary when we were being instructed by the priest for the Christian faith. He was a fairly young man and very passionate about his faith. We were almost at the end of the day when he asked the fifty or so students present if they had any grievance with the Christian church. My hand shot up, and I found myself briefly telling the story of how the Archbishop of Canterbury had told my real father not to have anything to do with my mother or myself after she had got pregnant with me. The young priest looked aghast, fell to his knees and raised his hands in the air, asking God to work through him so as to apologise to me. It was a very moving moment; there was not a dry eye in the house!

CHAPTER 37

AUGUST 2005. MY ORDINATION

The night arrived before my ordination. I had been on our last retreat down in Cornwall and had a long drive back to Gidia Park. When I arrived at my friends' house, where I had been temporarily staying, there was no one at home. I was tired and desperate to get myself ready for the next day. I therefore decided to book into a hotel round the corner. As soon as I had settled into my room, my mobile phone rang. It was my friends saying they had now returned home. As it was near 9pm, I decided to stay put where I was, in the hope of having a good night's sleep before the next day's Ordination. I took a shower, then to my horror found I could not turn off the taps. After a long struggle, the water started seeping into my room. I quickly got dressed to seek help, as reception was not responding to my phone calls!

Finally, I managed to get another room, my old

room now being under several inches of water. Around midnight I fell asleep, only to be woken up with a fire alarm ringing persistently. I dashed out of bed, ran out of my room, but no, there was no fire, just the alarm going off by mistake, I was informed. I went back to bed and got to thinking what all this was about. In a few hours, I was about to be Ordained in Kensington. So I started up a deep conversation with God. There really was nothing else to do in the middle of the night when sleep was hard to come by.

It came to me that God was showing me that life was not necessary going to be easy now that I was about to commit myself into full time service as a Minister. I would have to go through all sorts of events (fire and water) and still manage to be detached. This was the final act of learning the art of detachment. None of my immediate family came for my Ordination, except for my half-brother from my biological father's side; for that, I was very touched.

The art of detachment is a very worthwhile investment. It does not mean you cannot love or enjoy life. In fact, you can enjoy it even more, as you are no longer attached to any outcome. This brings enormous freedom and peace; I would recommend it to anyone. My life has changed since I started practicing non-attachment. It was not easy in the beginning. I would just about think I was there, when something or someone would tap me on the shoulder and say, "So you think you have managed non-attachment, do you? Well, how about this one?" And I would be sent reeling backwards again. But as each experience came and went, I noticed that the time of getting over the event lessened. One day, I discovered that a disturbance would happen but I could manage to sail through it quickly. Oh what joy to discover that I could let this event pass and not get upset or hooked into the drama. But I promise I won't become complacent. You just never know!

My Ordination was a holy event for me. I felt as if I had turned a corner, ready for another new beginning. I still had not found a place to live, so now it became urgent. I decided to head back to Suffolk. London was not working out, as I simply did not have enough money to buy a house that was suitable for my work.

First, I stayed with my dear friend Christine Johnson, who has since passed, but was a superb Reiki Healer. Through a friend of hers, I managed to rent a house in Aldeburgh. It was a lovely quiet time for me, walking by the sea every day. I had plenty of time to practice my meditation and catch up on reading, as well as look for a suitable property.

This was also a time searching for a house for

the Asha Centre. I had become very friendly with the AMAZING Zerbanoo Gifford, whose son, Mark, had also been one of my colleagues ordained as an Inter-Faith Minister. Zerbanoo was in the middle of writing her book called *The Secrets of the World's Inspirational Women*, which she kindly asked me to be in. The book was launched in the London Portrait Gallery, where a painting was hung of the women who had submitted their inspiring stories in Zerbanoo's book. I invited Sarah, Duchess of York, to come with me, and it was a very successful evening.

Moat Hall

CHAPTER 38

2006. LIFE IN MOAT HALL BEGINS ~ 15 YEARS IN LOVING SERVICE

Early Spring 2006, a house came on the market by the name of Moat Hall, in a little village called Darsham, in Suffolk. Although I at first did not want to view it, because I thought it too close to the A12, something prompted me to take a look anyway. The minute I entered the house, I knew it was what I had been looking for with the money I had available. Within two months, I moved in. I started to paint the house from top to bottom, had new carpets and curtains put in and was up and running in one month! How I managed to do all that work in such a short time is anyone's guess.

The first thing to organize was a Service. I had been holding Sai Baba Bhajan Services since my return to England in 2000, so I called upon all the people I knew who had attended. We had our first Service at Moat Hall on 6th May 2006. Ever since then, I have held Inter-Faith Services every first Sunday of the month. Moat Hall was such a perfect place for me to do my work in. There was a lovely large room set aside for an Inter-Faith Temple, as well as a beautiful large kitchen with gorgeous views, where everyone could enjoy their food. When it was cold, we would sit in the sitting room, in front of a huge inglenook fireplace and have Satsang. Many people came to stay for retreats, with four spare bedrooms available. I also had a room set aside for my clinic, with a large client list of people coming for allergy treatments and healing. Never once have I advertised my treatments. I believe that people are sent to me who need my help.

Ah yes, the allergy treatments. This was so incredible, as I was not about to do any more training. A lady came to do a retreat during the Christmas of 2006 and kept talking about a treatment she was giving at a school she owned for challenged children. She kept mentioning the word NAET. Eventually, I got curious and looked it up on the internet. NAET stands for Dr Nambudripad's Allergy Elimination Technique. It is the most profound treatment, that allows the human body to heal itself through the nerve endings of the spine that lead into the brain, as well as using acupuncture pressure points. Naturally, I *had* to train and took my first NAET course in May 2007. After four years of training, I have now become an advanced practitioner in NAET. My patients who come to have this treatment have exciting results. It is with such joy I have managed to incorporate this advanced treatment into my already existing healing work.

2008 saw my second sweet grandson born. Twice a year, my daughter and grandchildren used to come and stay, and we would have magical times together. They had my big garden to play in, as well as the seaside close by, where we used to go crabbing in Walbeswick most afternoons.

In 2008, a court in Turkey had brought charges against Sarah, Duchess of York over a controversial ITV documentary, in which she went undercover to secretly film the dreadful conditions of orphanages in Ankara and Istanbul. The courts accused her, in her absence, of going against the law in acquiring footage and violating the privacy of five children. The charges carried a jail term of more than 22 years. She had gone in disguise to visit the orphanages with her daughter Princess Eugenie, filming the children living in dreadful conditions. It was a sensitive time for Turkey, as they were in the middle of joining the European Union. Sara had also gone in disguise to Romania, accompanied by her other daughter Princess Beatrice, again filming similar orphans in distress.

When all this came to light, I got a call from Sarah, as she wanted to go back to India to speak with Sai Baba. In early September 2009, we met in Bangalore airport and drove down to Puttaparthi, where I had forewarned Sai Baba's secretary, dear Mr Chakravarthi, that we were coming for a short visit. We were graciously put up in Shanti Bhavan, the VIP accommodation in the Ashram. Sarah sat that night writing a letter to Baba, telling Him of her predicament about the court case, asking for His help. The next morning, we were ushered in to sit by the gate where Sai Baba appears from His abode.

It was during the time when Sai Baba would mostly come into the Temple being driven in His car and very few interviews were given. His car came out and did a quick round. When He came to where we were sitting, on His way out of the Temple, His car stopped by us, indicating for us to come and speak with Him. I let Sarah go up herself to His window, as this visit was for her in her urgent quest. She gave Baba her letter and spoke a few words with Him. As she spoke to Him, He was looking at me all the time. He then threw two of His handkerchiefs out the car window, which happened to land on the floor. Quickly, a lady sitting next to me got up and swiped one of them, before I saw Sarah bend down and pick up the other one. I told her afterwards to keep it, as Baba had wanted her to have it to wipe away her tears. When we got back to UK, shortly after our visit, the court case was dismissed. Another of Sai's miracles?

In 2009, Sarah and Andrew invited me to come and join them on a holiday in Spain, where they had rented a beautiful house for the summer. It was a most interesting time, but it will stay private.

CHAPTER 39

2010. ANOTHER VISIT TO SAI BABA'S ASHRAM

February 2010 saw me back in Sai Baba's Ashram. I had such a beautiful time there, in fact one of my best. I had come to thank Sai Baba for once again saving my youngest grandson's life. He had contracted a dreadful disease that eats at bones in the body and was hospitalised. I had written to my dear Sai Sister Raghuvir, who was very close to Baba, asking if she could ask Him to send help. She did so and was given some coconuts to offer the Lord Ganesh statue at the main gate into the Ashram. Three days later, my daughter informed me that her son was cured! Thank You Beloved Baba.

So there I was, sitting in the Temple, with a special card I had bought for Baba, in the hope that He would take it as He passed me. Inside the card was a big red heart with the words "I Love YOU", and on the other side of the card it read, "I love you more than chocolate." I had also written in my own writing,

"Beloved Baba, please tell me what You will have me do for You." As Baba entered the Temple in His wheelchair, as by now He could no longer walk very well, He came to me and gave me His beautiful smile, taking my letter, again blessing my hands.

Later in the day, I got a message from a Sai Brother that my dear Sai Sister Raghuvir wanted to see me. In the spur of the moment, I asked if I could bring my friend and lawyer, Sukhjit Ahluwalia, and it was agreed he could come as well. I realise now that she had wanted someone to be there to witness what was about to transpire. So it was we came to her flat that evening. We sat for a long time talking about her Divine experiences with Sai Baba. She was so fortunate to have been given a flat right opposite the men's entrance gate to the Temple; that way, she could always see Sai Baba when He was sitting in His chair. She told us that she had written the Sri Sathya Sai Sathya Narayana Katha, a booklet of fourteen pages chronicling Baba's life, which Baba Himself had blessed. Several copies had been printed and blessed by Baba personally, as well as a photo taken of Him reading the Katha. She told us that whoever was given one of the blessed booklets, as well as the photo, would be allowed to read the Katha in public. She then gave me a pair of silver padukas, a silver mug, a silver container with Baba's cloves and cardamom in, as well as the booklet and photo of Baba reading the booklet.

We left Sister's apartment late that evening, escorted back to our accommodations by a Sevadal. I could hardly sleep that night for the energy in my room and fell asleep vowing that I would do my best to read 85 public readings of the sacred booklet for Baba's upcoming 85th Birthday, which was nine months away.

When I got back to UK, I held my first public reading of the Sai Katha on the 16th February. I took a photo of the people attending, making a recording in a special album I had bought for the purpose of recording each reading, of which I had dedicated 85 for Sai Baba's 85th birthday that year. Without knowing the outcome, on 23rd November 2010, the 85th Sri Sathya Sai Narayana Katha was read at Moat Hall in front of 27 Sai devotees, who had come to celebrate Sai Baba's birthday. A month later, I went back to Baba's Ashram and brought the album with the recorded events of the public readings to show Him. To my great delight, Baba blessed the album and was very pleased with the effort, which was nothing short of a huge humble experience for me, to offer Him with all my heart.

It was wonderful being back in the Ashram to spend Christmas there. I had been before at Christmas time, as it was always the best place to be during this time, celebrating the birth of beloved Lord Jesus. On the morning of 24th December, just before going to the Temple for morning prayers, I said a little prayer to Baba in front of a picture of Jesus I had placed on the altar in my bedroom. I lit a little four-hour tealight, and as I did, I asked Baba this question: "Baba, are You and Jesus the same person?" When I got back after lunch, the tealight was still alight! When I went to bed that night, it was still alight! I fell asleep and woke up around midnight to a huge light illuminating my room from the tiny candle, which was still alight! When I got up in the morning, the candle was still burning! I left for morning prayers, and when I got back, as I opened my front door, I saw the candle go out and a big cloud of smoke arose from it. What do you think the answer for my prayer meant?

Vibhuti on Jesus picture

On 24th April 2011, Easter Sunday of that year, my Beloved Guru Sri Sathya Sai Baba left His body and went into Samadhi. He had taken four weeks to prepare His devotees that He was leaving us. If He had gone suddenly, it would have been too big a shock for many. For me it was a big wrench, but at the same time, Sai Baba had taught me, right from the beginning of my meeting Him, to always find Him inside myself. For that I am truly grateful, as I am able to forge a beautiful continuous relationship with Him now that He is no longer walking the earth, continuing His Mission from the other side. I still have beautiful dreams of Him from time to time, as well as deep conversations when needed.

2012. MOAT HALL

So here I sit, in my lovely kitchen at Moat Hall, looking out on the snowy landscape, thinking I have come a long way on my holy journey. I have been through a lot, ever since early childhood, but I have come through it. I am happy, well-adjusted and feel a wonderful sense of peace. I love helping people get better in their body, mind and spirit, and I believe I am good at what I do. It is interesting to note, that not once since becoming a therapist and healer have I promoted myself. All the people who have come to me for treatments have been through recommendations or simply sent to me by the universe, or is it by Sai Baba?

How did I manage to get through this rather unusual life? I cannot imagine that I have earnt all this latter good fortune because of my actions in this lifetime. Maybe it has been earned in a previous life? I now believe we also start clearing the way for a better life when we awaken to our inner purpose, when the ego gets a chance to collapse.

So what is it that affords me this grace? Am I reaping the benefits of the service that my biological father did for humanity in his lifetime, as well as his love for God? If so, I feel the blessing and would not change a thing! Is God being kind to me because I forgave so easily my father, mother, uncle, husband, sister, daughter, etc? To me they were just my greatest teachers. With humility I can say that they brought me a great gift; the gift was to allow me to forgive them at the deepest level and love them unconditionally. Is that the secret then? Maybe it is. Or maybe it was because I was willing to change myself into becoming a better person, diving ever deeper into compassion, by going BEYOND FORGIVENESS.

Casting yourself at God's feet in helpless desperation is all well and good, but taking action and *responsibility* at your end is essential. Prayer is a relationship with God, but half the job is yours. The benefit of prayer is in the asking.

I just want God. I want to feel God inside me. I want God to play in my blood stream, the way dolphins amuse themselves in the ocean. I want to become drunk on the word of the Beloved. I would love for God to become fashionable again!

I would like to thank Sai Baba, and myself, for arriving at this place of peace, for having the courage to keep going, with utter faith that something bigger than myself is looking after me and that I have been led to that Greatness. Beloved Sai Baba, you helped me heal myself back to wholeness. May I spend the rest of my life being of service to Your vision for the world, that Goodness will prevail and we will all have peace on earth before too long. With Your divine message on our lips: "LOVE ALL, SERVE ALL - HELP EVER, HURT NEVER."

Thank you, God, for helping me to know that all that I seek is coming to me now. Thank you, God, for allowing me to feel right now the peace that comes with gratitude for what is, replacing the yearning for what was not. Thank you for bringing me to the understanding that from this *isness* comes all that is now not, but surely will be. Let me stay then in the *isness that is You.*

The search for God is a reversal of the normal mundane worldly order. In the search for God, you revert from what attracts you and swim towards that which is difficult. You abandon your comforting and familiar habits, with the hope that something greater will be offered to you in return for what you've given up. Every religion in the world operates on the same common understandings of what it means to be a good disciple. Get up early in the morning and pray to your God, hone your virtues, be a good neighbour, respect yourself and others, master your cravings. We all agree it would be easier to sleep in, and many of us do! But for millennia there have been others who choose instead to get up before the sun and wash their faces and go to their prayers.

The devout of this world perform their rituals without guarantee that anything good will ever come of it. There are of course plenty of scriptures and plenty of priests who make plenty of promises as to what your good work will yield (or threats as to the punishments awaiting you if you lapse), but to even believe all this is an act of faith, because nobody amongst us is shown the end game.

Devotion is diligence without assurance. Faith is a way of saying, "Yes, I pre-accept the terms of the universe and I embrace in advance what I am presently incapable of understanding." There's a reason we refer to 'leaps of faith', because the decision to consent to any notion of divinity is a mighty jump from the rational, over to the unknowable. I don't care how diligently scholars of every religion will try to sit you down with their stacks of books and prove to you through scripture that their faith is indeed rational: it isn't. If faith were rational, it wouldn't be, by definition, faith. Faith is belief in what you cannot see or prove or touch. Faith is walking face first and full speed into the dark. If we truly knew all the answers in advance as to the meaning of life and the nature of God and the destiny of our souls, our belief would not be a leap of faith, it would not be a courageous act of humanity, it would be ... a prudent insurance policy!

I am assuming custodial responsibility for the maintenance of my own soul, going BEYOND FORGIVENESS and arriving at that place in my soul which always comes from a place of LOVE and settles in PEACE.

LOVE ALL SERVE ALL

Sai Baba's Letter: 19th February 1997
(the letter that changed my life.)

My dear Children
AWAKE! AWAKE! AWAKE!

There is no time for slumber. You have been asleep and dreaming for thousands of lifetimes. If you do not awake now, this chance may not come again for thousands more.

Come with me, separation is no longer the order of the day. I separated myself from myself so that I could love myself more. The experience is finished. I want all of myself to return and merge into me, the ONE SELF.

*I gave many of you the advantage of an **unhappy childhood, including conflict or separation from your mother and father.** In doing this, I removed from you the temptation to become attached to human parents or a specific family situation; that left you with only one option, that is to 'attach yourself to me'.*

Why do you not avail yourself of this opportunity instead of continually seeking these relationships that can never satisfy you? Even if your childhood has been idyllic as you would have liked, it is not your mother's love you need.

*Ultimately, it is not even the love of this Name and Form (Baba) that you long for. Your deepest, innermost urge is to return to yourself – to love yourself to become the **Being**, the **Awareness** and the **Bliss**, which is all you will ever be.*

Let go of the past, stop trying to get from each other what you still think you missed from childhood or marriage. You will never find anyone who is enough; not even Me.

Love yourself, know yourself – Only you will ever be enough!

Can you not love yourself because I love you over and over again? Did I not virtually move heaven and earth to bring you to me? I have asked all my devotees to repeat the mantra "I AM GOD, I AM NOT DIFFERENT FROM GOD."

Now I ask you specifically to follow that instruction; it will be more helpful than any other thing you can do.

Now remember, that I love you – love yourself.

BABA

CHAPTER 40

2012. A TURNING POINT

Aha! So you thought this was the end of my story, but it is not. Now comes an even bigger challenge for me to overcome, in truly finding *forgiveness at the deepest level*. So hold on to your seats and enjoy this extraordinary ride of history in the making.

It is now May 2020. Much has happened. It has been a divine, peaceful time at Moat Hall, but also much hard work, keeping this beautiful Spiritual Healing Centre going, but I have loved and enjoyed every golden moment.

I will attempt to report the latest in the intervening years. Covid19 arrived in UK at the beginning of the year, and everything seems to have changed regarding our daily lives. It is now lockdown, so a perfect time to catch up with my story to date! I contracted double pneumonia in April, which was diagnosed by one of the Sai Devotee Doctors, who came to my services. I suffered greatly but refused to go into hospital. I kept saying, "Sai, you are my doctor, you are my healer, please look after me." After 2 months, I started feeling more normal.

Since 2012, when I last wrote the story of my life to be published one day, but instinctively knew there would be a truly sensational ending, much has transpired again. Up until 2015 I was busy running my Healing Spiritual Centre here at Moat Hall, where I have lived since 2006. After training to become an Allergy and Trauma Specialist, I had a busy life treating hundreds of people with considerable success. I absolutely loved my work, as finally I was getting great results quickly, helping people get rid of their ailments. I held retreats for groups of people a few times a year, as well as individual ones. I also loved playing my Tibetan singing bowls and used them for healing.

Suddenly in 2012, it was announced on the news that a Nuclear Power Station in Leiston, Suffolk, was considered for application and that all the fields surrounding my home, Moat Hall, were to be earmarked for a Park & Ride, for over 1000 cars and coaches, accommodating the staff constructing the Nuclear Power station of Sizewell C in Leiston.

With great trepidation, I contacted an estate agent, but was told that, until a firm decision was made by the government, there would be no chance of selling my home; it had now become blighted! I had no choice but to sit back and wait to see what would transpire.

My love for Sai Baba had followed me ever since I first met Him in 1994, and many miracles had happened for me, through Him. I was running my home as an official Sai Centre for the Sri Sathya Sai International Organization and had been Chair for East Suffolk since 2009. I now had to trust that Sai Baba had everything under control.

ENTER SONJA VENTURI

During my visit in 2010 to Prasanthi Nilayam (Sai Baba's Ashram in Puttaparthi, South India), which was His last Christmas with us in His body form, I met a lawyer and devotional singer by the name of Sonja Venturi. She was the main singer in the Christmas concert that year. A few days earlier, I had been out in the village when I heard music coming from a shop. I was mesmerized by the voice that was singing and wanted to buy the CD. As the shopkeeper had a fake copy of the CD, he was unable to tell me the name of the singer. But I persuaded him to sell me the CD anyway. So when Sonja started singing that evening in front of Sai Baba, I recognized it as the voice on the CD!

Later, I invited Sonja to come to Moat Hall Sai Centre to sing for my group of people, who gather once a month in the Temple, for an Inter-Faith Service. Our

Beloved Sai Baba had passed away on the 24th April that year. Most devotees were reeling from the loss. So when Sonja finally turned up with her musicians at the end of September, it was a great blessing for everyone. Sonja loved being at Moat Hall, where she felt safe and comfortable. The following year, she came again for a Summer Retreat lasting three days. That was when Vibhuti (holy ash) again started appearing on Sai Baba's pictures in the Temple, even on the speakers, as well as in many of the rooms at Moat Hall. We were thrilled with this turn of events and continued working together from time to time.

It had always been a dream of Sonja's to visit Scotland, so in 2013, I decided during the summer holidays to drive up there with her in tow. We arrived in Oban, then taking the ferry over to Mull Island. It was so nice seeing Sonja enjoy the boat ride, as she had never done anything like that before. Arriving in Mull, we took a coach across the island and arrived at the tiny boat landing for Iona Island. The crossing was rough but quick, and soon we were installed in a cosy hotel, yards from the boat landing.

Iona is the most sacred place to visit. I had been there on my own, during my studies to become an Inter-Faith Minister. We joined the service in the evening up at the Abbey, which was magical, with many musicians playing. The following evening we again went to the Abbey, being served a holy supper by candlelight.

After our trip to Iona, we motored down to Fortingall, 8 miles from Aberfeldy, where I had stayed with my Reiki Master, who had initiated me into a Reiki Master. The energy in Fortingall is powerful. It lies at the entrance to the mystical Glen Lyon, which is where I had once wanted to buy a house to set up my Spiritual Healing Centre. One of the things which makes Fortingall historical is the oldest living yew tree, situated next to the little church by the Fortingall Hotel, which I had also considered buying on my travels to Scotland when I was searching for a place to live.

Life continued at Moat Hall, doing my best at all times, looking after the big house and garden. I was doing lots of treatments, as well as looking after people wanting to come for retreats. I tended to only have the heating on when people came to stay, so it was no surprise when one night I had a sweet dream of my Sai Baba, who appeared looking a bit worried. I asked Him if I could take Padnamaskar (touching of the Holy Feet). He indicated to do so by lifting His Robe to reveal His Feet; lo and behold, they were covered in ski socks! When I told of my dream to the people gathered for my next Service, one lady piped up, "Well, Leonora, it is rather cold here in the winter months."

Another incident worth mentioning is when a doctor and his family came to see me in great distress, as a court case was imminent, giving a bad reputation to the doctor, which was truly unfounded. We were talking in the hall by the front door, where a photo of Sai Baba was hanging with His arms in blessing, which had a light above it. The family were all in tears and said they were worried sick for the forthcoming court case. I told them that they had to have full faith and trust that Sai Baba would look after them for the details of the outcome. If they did not believe this was so, they were not fully surrendered to Him and they were demonstrating that Sai would not look after the case. With that, the light above Sai Baba's picture started flickering on and off three times. The crying stopped and the family went away happy, as Sai had demonstrated that He was with them and knew every detail of their predicament. Needless to say, when the court case was heard, it was dismissed almost immediately by the judge.

CHAPTER 41

2014. ENTER SADGURU MADHUSUDAN SAI - SATHYA SAI GRAMA MUDDENAHALLI ASHRAM, BANGALORE, INDIA

In 2014, Sonja and I were invited to a Sai Centre in Chicago, USA, for her to do a concert and for me to give a talk on my experiences with Sai Baba. It was there we heard of a phenomenon that was happening in one of Sai Baba's Ashrams, called Muddenahalli, surrounded by the Nandi Hills, 30 minutes outside Bangalore. It was a place that Sai Baba would stay a few times a year when He was alive. A place where all the teachers were *Thyaga Jeevis* (which means renunciants).

Apparently, a former student of Sai Baba's, named Madhusudan Naidu, had been having visions of Sai Baba, starting shortly after His passing. In fact, Sai Baba would appear in Madhusudan's room and sit and talk to him (further reading of this phenomenon can be found in Madhusudan's first book, *The Story Divine, Part 1: Living with God*).

Sai Baba would then instruct Madhusudan to start building schools for the poor rural children in the district of Karnataka. To date, twenty-two schools have been erected, one more magnificent than the other. There is also a University for Human Excellence that has been built. There, many of the students are being trained to become the future teachers for the twenty-two rural schools established so far. Five Children Heart Hospitals have been built. Tens of thousands of heart operations have been performed there. Sai Baba also wanted Ashrams to be set up in eighteen different countries, ready for when His third incarnation "Prema Sai" would start traveling around the world, teaching the meaning of life.

This was also the time when my daughter without warning, wrote me a very hard, unfortunate email, saying she never wanted to speak to me again.

By 2014, Madhusudan was told by Sai Baba to go public, explaining that he was being guided by Sai Baba to continue His Mission until 2021, when it had originally been predicted that Sai Baba would no longer be amongst us in His body. So it was that I got to hear about this unprecedented account of a divine adventure of saga, service and surrender; a tale of tangible transformation and a testimony to the power of faith that was about to take place.

Then, that **Voice** that would sometimes speak to me spoke to me when I was mowing the lawns at Moat Hall (I always love meditating when mowing the lawns), shortly after I had heard about the amazing story about Madhusudan. It said, "How about offering your home to Me and we will make it into an Ashram for Prema Sai?"

I was mystified, as I had no idea how that was to come about. I was more than willing but needed to find out how to go about it!

I contacted Sonja, to ask if she knew of anyone I could write to, re-offering my home as an Ashram. It was decided I should get in touch with the head warden of Muddenahalli Ashram, Sri B.N. Narasimha Murthy, to ask him if he would ask Sai Baba via Madhusudan if I had heard correctly, that I should offer my home to be turned into a Prema Sai Ashram.

On 11th August 2015, I wrote to Narasimha Murthy Sir. I got an answer back via email on 12th August from him. He wrote that Baba was touched by my noble gesture and please could I get in touch with the Chair of the London Trust, which had been set up to support one of the schools being built in India, for him to come and view Moat Hall.

15th August, The Chair and his wife came to

view Moat Hall. We also viewed my neighbours 6-acre property, which was up for sale, which, in combination with Moat Hall, would make an excellent Ashram for Sai Baba's Mission. The Chair said he would write to Narasimha Murthy Sir to tell him of his visit.

On 24th August, I received an email from The Chair to say that he'd had a conversation with Narasimha Murthy Sir and that Moat Hall should go into the London Trust, but I could remain there to do my spiritual work! I wrote back to him saying that before such a thing could happen, I would like to have an interview with Madhusudan so that I could be 100% sure that it was Sai Baba working through Madhusudan. This was arranged for the upcoming visit in September, with the entourage coming from Muddenahali.

1st September: what an extraordinary day that was. I had invited Sonja Venturi and three members of my Sai Bhajan group to accompany me. We arrived in London and went to the house of the London Trust Chair, where Madhusudan and his entourage, who had travelled with him, were staying. We were lead into the Interview room by KR, who is also an ex-student of Sri Sathya Sai Baba's school in Brindavan, just outside Bangalore, and has been in Muddenahalli since 2011, dedicating his entire life to the ongoing Divine Mission of Sai Baba.

As I entered the Interview Room, Madhusudan was sitting crossed-legged by Sai Baba's designated empty chair. Supposedly, Sai Baba was speaking through Madhusudan. He asked me to give him the letter I had brought, offering my home and its contents, including the folder with the pictures of my house. He looked at the pictures, smiled and asked me if I was sure I wanted to offer my house to the ongoing Mission of Sai Baba. I told him I was honoured and delighted to do so. He also said that the London Trust would try to purchase my neighbour's property to enable us to have a larger Ashram.

I was told many things about my life, as well as dealings I'd had with Sai Baba whilst He was alive that were only personal to me. This was very reassuring. I felt I could trust this sweet soul and the people around him. So it was, I offered everything I owned at the Divine Feet of Sri Sathya Sai Baba, through Madhusudan. The atmosphere in the room was electrifying. I felt peaceful and that I was being guided in doing the right thing. Just before leaving the room, Madhusudan gave me a large pendulum with Sai Baba's picture on it hanging from a large gold chain, which has since been greatly admired by hundreds of people.

There was to be an event that evening for around 200 people. Madhusudan had asked me if I was comfortable with him announcing that I had offered my home to Sai Baba's Ongoing Mission to become the UK Ashram for Prema Sai. There was absolutely no hesitation or doubt in my heart that I was not doing the right thing. I felt strongly that God wanted me to do this. It felt as if Sai Baba had chosen another practical way to let me serve Him, with no rewards expected by me whatsoever. Maybe this was what all the struggles had prepared me for? Maybe this was my soul's salvation? It almost became knowledge to me that life is not futile; that the way to enlightenment was to offer everything to God; that this was possibly the way for the ultimate experience. By acknowledging my shortfalls and admitting to my weaknesses, I was watching them move into my greatest strength.

Before the evening event started, KR came up to me and said that Madhusudan wanted to make sure I felt absolutely comfortable about the public announcement. I looked into this sweet soul's eyes and said, "I am absolutely sure I want to offer my home to His Mission."

The following morning, I arrived at The Chair's house to talk with the London Trustees about the logistics of offering my home, Moat Hall, to Sai Baba's Mission out of Muddenahalli, and also to secure a future for myself. I invited Sonja Venturi to come with me, as she was now acting as my official lawyer, to find a solution as to how to hand over Moat Hall to the Sai Mission. We sat down with Narasimha Murthy Sir and the London Trustees to discuss the logistics.

In the afternoon, we went in for a second Interview. During this Interview, Madhusudan told me that since I had split from my husband, I had turned fully towards God. He also said that for a long time I had wanted to set up an official Ashram for Sai Baba. He went on to say that Sai Baba had found Moat Hall for me all those years ago, specifically for this purpose, and had been finetuning it for the past nine years. He said that the property next door would become available for us and it would be part of the Ashram! He mentioned that I'd had many ups and downs during my life, with sometimes enormous wealth and other times nothing. He said that I was very different from the rest of my family, with a lot of jealousy from them. It was also revealed that Sonja had been my daughter in a past life and this was the reason why she was always concerned for me. On leaving the Interview Room, he gave me a box of chocolates and said, "Baba knows you love chocolates, but only one a day." This amazed me, as I had asked Baba for ages to make me strong and only eat one chocolate a day. The last card I had given Him in Prasanthi Nilayam Ashram before His passing had said inside, "I love you more than chocolate."

When I got back to Moat Hall from London, I started preparing for the exciting prospect of making my home into a Prema Sai Ashram. I was so happy and excited, moving forward by an invisible hand that was giving me strength to do all that had to be done, with no doubts arising, just blind faith that this was the ultimate blessing.

A few emails went back and forth between myself and Sri Narasimha Murthy, Madhusudan's right-hand spokesperson, who had been a Sai Devotee since the age of 19, dedicating his entire life to Sai Baba. He was also the warden of Sai Baba's Ashram in Muddenahalli, 30 minutes outside Bangalore. Sai Baba would stay there when He used to visit Bangalore and had great affection for this holy place.

The story goes that when Madhusudan started getting direct messages from Sai Baba, after Baba left His body on 24th April 2011, he contacted Narasimha Murthy Sir to tell him about his experiences of witnessing Sai Baba in His subtle form. Apparently, Narasimha Murthy was totally convinced that in fact it must be so, because when they met for the first time, Madhusudan started telling him many private things that had happened between Sai Baba and Narasimha Murthy that only they both knew about. A deep relationship sprang up between them, and Madhusudan was invited to come and live in Muddenahalli.

On 16th September 2015, I'd still heard nothing back from the London Trust, so I wrote an email to them, asking when we would hear from them. I got an email back that evening saying that because they used a pro bono lawyer, we'd have to fit in with their timing.

As the days went by, I concentrated on getting Moat Hall ready to look its best, for the hopeful eventuality of it officially being inaugurated into an Ashram. It was a question of full trust and surrender.

There was a leak in the conservatory roof which had to be seen to. I also stripped the wallpaper in my small office and had it re-papered. If I woke up tired in the morning, I'd hear the Voice say, "Get up, there is much to do." So I jumped up with gladness in my heart and soldiered on. Sometimes, I wished that I could have help from other Sai devotees, but at other times, I loved the silence, just getting on with doing what needed to be done.

On 28th September, I got an email from a Maria Parker of Burtons Solicitors, who strongly recommended that I should create a Life Interest Trust for myself, for my property during my lifetime, as it was only in very exceptional circumstances that they would recommend or would ever advise a client to transfer their principal residence into someone else's Trust during a lifetime! After this, the communication went dead between the London Trust and myself.

On 7th October, I got an email from Narasimha Murthy to say that I was to make arrangements for Madhusudan to visit Moat Hall on the 2nd and 3rd April 2016, when Moat Hall was to be inaugurated into Sai Grace Ashram, as well as arrange a public Satsang close to my house for around 200 people. Narasimha Murthy had been in talks with the London Trust to expedite the process of transfer of my property, so that all expenses connected with the Ashram could be borne by them. But as nothing had been arranged with them, I bore all the expenses myself, again with gladness in my heart. My mantra daily was, "Baba, I love You, I am here, I am willing to serve You. Please let me know what You will have me do."

At the end of October, I got another email from Narasimha Murthy saying that he had submitted the contents of my emails at the Lotus Feet of Swami. His instructions were:

- Stay in touch with your neighbour, as eventually this house will also be Swami's property.
- The Sai Centre people can continue to come for Satsang, but not for discussing the issue of donation of Moat Hall.

-   Prepare an estimate for the works to be done at Moat Hall. The expenses will be met by London Trust once the property is registered in the name of the Trust, as that is a legal requirement.

He ended by saying that they looked forward to being at Moat Hall with Swami on my birthday in April 2026.

So now it was pretty clear to me that all would proceed and my dream of offering my home to become an Ashram would become a reality. Day and night I worked to get everything ready. It was hard work, with many expenses and still no word about the London Trust coming on board to help. It must have been Sai Baba's will! I was happy and content anyway, as I was fortunate that my therapy work brought in the money to cover the new heavy costs for the April arrival. But at the last moment, I got a personal cheque from the London Chair to cover the expenses for the new roof of the conservatory. I was very grateful.

On 16th February 2016, I got an email from Narasimha Murthy to say that the forthcoming stay had now been cut down to one night's stay instead of the original two, as the London Chair had prayed to Madhusudan that he and the entourage should stay in his residence to rest!

On 2nd April 2016, Madhusudan and his entourage

from Muddenahalli, including Isaac Tigrett, as well as the London Trustees and their wives, arrived to inaugurate my home into the official title of Sai Grace Ashram. I had been extremely busy preparing for their stay, as well as a public event for nearly 250 people in a beautiful local venue the following day. Madhusudan and his assistant, Bhuvana, who was also an ex-Sai student, stayed in the now to be inaugurated Sai Grace Ashram. It was a joy to get to know this special soul Madu, as we called him, away from the crowds. We had a beautiful private Satsang in the Temple for about twenty-five people, followed by a delicious dinner prepared by the Italian Sai team. After dinner, I was called into the Temple, where all the London Trustees were sitting, as well as Madhusudan and his entourage. Madhusudan created a beautiful ring of the nine planets for me and told me I was to become a trustee of the London Trust. I was not sure I could see joy on some of the faces of the Trustees.

In the morning, Madhusudan came down the stairs and asked if I would show him around the house and garden. He explained to me that the day before, he had not seen anything, as he was in the presence of Sai Baba and in a trance state. This sweet, humble soul was truly a delight to be in the presence of. I could feel the difference in the house. It seemed to be infused with a very special energy, which was tangible. I could not see Sai Baba myself, but I felt His heightened presence through Madhusudan. After breakfast, several people arrived for private Interviews.

The afternoon was in full swing, getting ready for the Inauguration. KR was rushing around at the hired venue, making sure that all was arranged to his satisfaction, but saw too late that the cushion on Sai Baba's Chair was missing. Since then, we have both often talked about this omission, as shown in the now famous photo taken by Gabriella Campomizzi, with Madhusudan reverently bowing down by Sai Baba's Chair, in submission to his Master, minus the cushion. KR has assured me that we have been forgiven! Sonja Venturi had the blessings to play on the magnificent Steinway piano, which graced the beautiful hall, and what a magical journey she took us on, with her soulful singing and playing of the piano.

How happy and blessed I felt, standing on the stage, announcing to all the people present that I was offering my home to the ongoing Sai Mission. It was offered with a totally pure heart, with absolutely no ulterior motive. I was now going to be the custodian of Sai Grace Ashram, holding the space for all who visited in the future to learn about the teachings of our great Inter-Faith Master of all times, Sri Sathya Sai Baba, to be followed in the future by Prema Sai's presence.

After the Inauguration, I was called in for an Interview with Madhusudan. I invited Sonja Venturi to come with me, as I wanted to discuss the logistics about the future of Sai Grace Ashram, and with Sonja being a lawyer, it seemed the perfect solution to have her join us. Sonja was trying to secure my future by saying that I should have enough security, that I would be looked after until my dying day. But Madhusudan insisted, "No lawyer," stating that the London Trust would look after me!

The following month, I was invited to join Madhusudan in Kodaikanal Tamil Nadu up in the cool mountains, where Sai Baba used to take His students during the hot month of May. That year there were 190 guests invited, as well as 25 boy students and 35 girl students. It was magical staying there, and I saw a softer side of Madhusudan. It was during this stay that Isaac Tigrett, who was also a guest, was heard saying that the Chair of the London Trust was not happy that he'd had to spend some money for the new conservatory roof at Sai Grace Ashram. He even said that I had changed my mind about giving my home for the Sai Mission. When later that day I was told about this, confirmed by not one but two girlfriends, I was very upset and immediately sent an email to Narasimha Murthy to tell him this was unacceptable and I wanted to speak with Madhusudan. He wrote back "how unfortunate" that Isaac had said that and "Swami" would see me in the morning for an Interview. Sonja and my girlfriend, Dona, being her first Interview, were also invited to attend this Interview. Madhusudan was so kind and sweet and told me he would have words with Isaac. He told me to just carry on with my work at Sai Grace, with Sai Baba's help, and that Dona and Sonja were to support me as well, and to let the London Trust in the meantime get on with what they were doing.

On 27th May, on my return to UK, I wrote an email to the Chair of the London Trust to explain what Madhusudan had said in Kodaikanal in front of Sonja and Dona, as well as saying I would pay him back the £10,000 if and when the opportunity arose. He wrote back to say that this was not necessary. But I vowed to myself, if I could, I would pay him back. I also got an email from Narasimha Murthy to say not to pay back the money (to date, I have paid him back £5000).

As the weeks went by, trying, on several occasions, to get in touch with the London Trust to formalize the handover, I came up against a brick wall, as if they were not really interested in helping moving things forward. It became rather frustrating, but I kept faith that all would be well in the end.

In November, I was invited to come to Muddenahalli Ashram, where I had been given a beautiful flat to be my home away from home. Madhusudan said that Swami had informed him that, as I had offered my home to Him, He was now offering a home to me. Truly, I was happy to have this beautiful place to call my home; flat number E405. Over the next couple of years, I spent precious time in getting my flat looking lovely, installing a nice kitchen so I could cook my own food when I wanted.

I had a sweet solo Interview with Madhusudan, saying how happy he was with me, and he blessed me profusely. He also announced that he would be coming back to the UK next April and would stay at Sai Grace for two days. I asked if I should finish writing my autobiography that Sai Baba had told me to start when He had blessed my hands in Prasanthi Nilayam, and Madhusudan confirmed that I should. I also plucked up the courage and asked if I would ever see my daughter again, as she had cut all communications with me. There was a long pause, then he looked at me and said, "No." Strangely, this revelation was softened when I walked out of the Interview Room and down the stairs to see KR son, who had come to pick me up from the Hilltop Residence after my Interview and driven me back to my flat.

On 14th November, I received an email from Madhusudan saying that "Swami would be coming next April to Sai Grace, only for me, and the rest is incidental." He wrote that he would spend enough time to clarify the future of Sai Grace and wanted Dona, my girlfriend, to be present as well.

On 30th November, I received an email from Madhusudan himself saying that, further to his advice in Muddenahalli, I was not to spend on changing anything more in Sai Grace. Prior to this, a new roof in the conservatory had been put in place, paid for by the Chair, by Madhusudan's command. I'd also had some new windows installed, as well as a new temple door leading out into the garden. The driveway was also extended, mostly paid for by donations of sweet generous Sai Devotees.

On 29th January 2017, Madhusudan sent an email to say he would soon send the right person to help me write my autobiography.

On 27th February 2017, I was again back in Muddenahalli. I was called for an Interview with my dear friend Kaya Günata, his assistant Taya, as well as Sonja Venturi. Madhusudan asked me to help Kaya with the details of the inauguration of the soon to be Turkish Ashram. I was thrilled to bits. I had earlier told Kaya that I had offered my home to become the

UK Ashram, which gave Kaya the incentive to get in contact with Madhusudan to re-offer his land in Turkey, which he had originally offered to Sai Baba in Prasanthi Nilayam in 1996.

During this Interview, Madhusudan also said he would like Sai Grace Ashram to move to a larger place, maybe closer to London (as my neighbour's property had been sold to someone else) and that I would be shown the piece of land on his next visit in April (nice to have witnesses to this conversation). Straight after the Interview, I bumped into the London Trust Chair and told him the news, excitedly expressing my desire for us both to work as a team to get the new, bigger Ashram realized. But I noticed a lack of enthusiasm from him!

3rd April 2017, exactly one year after the inauguration of Sai Grace, saw the land inauguration of the Turkish Ashram, by Madhusudan and his entourage, initiated by my Sai devotee friend of twenty years, Kaya Günata. It was thrilling to be asked to help with this special event, and the memories from this trip are truly never to be forgotten. It was here that Madhusudan asked me again to start looking for larger premises to relocate Sai Grace Ashram, as Moat Hall had outgrown us. In front of witnesses, he also asked me if I would like to by land with a house or land to build an Ashram on it. He also told me to apply for

Charity Status for Sai Grace, which I duly did when I got back to UK.

After my trip to Turkey, I had less than a week to get ready for the arrival of Madhusudan and his entourage on 11th April to stay in Sai Grace Ashram, while hosting another big public event for 250 people in a big venue one mile from the Ashram. I must have caught a bug on the plane coming back from Turkey, as the day of arrival dawned alongside a temperature and sore throat.

Rushing about getting the venue ready, with only one hour to do it in on the day, I lost my cool and shouted at the few volunteers, who were standing about chatting. I have apologised since for this outburst, but isn't it fascinating how people always remember you for your once-in-a-while outbursts instead of allowing for compassion and understanding? Maybe you have a trillion things to do and a set time to do it in? It was always me having to organize everything myself, and it was a humongous job. This had always been the case when I had a big event going on, as I was isolated at Sai Grace and there were very few people really willing to help. But the event went beautifully, and everyone was happy and content with the opportunity to be in the presence of Madhusudan, bringing Sai Baba's golden energy with him, as well as the always superb concert that Sonja Venturi rendered for us. For me, it has always been a huge opportunity to realize that I am capable of organizing big events; for that I am humbled and grateful.

The next morning, I was waiting for an Interview to discuss all aspects of Sai Grace Ashram, etc. In fact, if you remember, Madhusudan had written to me before he'd arrived, saying, "This visit is just for you and everything else is incidental." So there I was, exhausted, not having slept much because of my fever, but hopeful that a useful Interview was eminent.

I had been made aware that Madhusudan and his entourage were to leave no later than 10am, as they had a gruelling trip to bless four different homes across UK before returning to London in the evening. As 10am neared, I got more and more agitated, seeing one person after the other going in for Interviews. I was beginning to lose my cool again. By the time I finally got in for an Interview, Sonja came as well.

Madhusudan asked me to sit in a chair, and Sonja was asked to sit on the floor, next to where Madhusudan was sitting on the floor by Sai Baba's chair. He asked me how I was, and I replied rather harshly, "Not too happy."

"Oh," he said, "Why not?"

I proceeded to say that I was under the impression

we had arranged to have several meetings together to sort out the future of Sai Grace Ashram.

Madhusudan took offence at my tone, turned to Sonja and said, "Is this the way she talks to God?"

Poor Sonja, she just wanted to disappear into the floor, and she sat with her eyes averted from us both. Then she said almost in a whisper, "Please make her happy. She is sick and exhausted."

Madhusudan said, "I will try."

I of course was in floods of tears by now and asked to be excused to get a tissue from the en-suit bathroom. After getting a tissue, I returned to the room immediately.

Slowly, I collected myself and we talked about a few things. I have a recording of this interview, but it was evident that I was not really in a fit state to have a constructive conversation. I could hear myself saying that I thought this visit was to be solely for meetings about Sai Grace.

Madhusudan proceeded to say, "I have to speak to people to soften them up, to get them to give what I want." We parted on good terms. (Here, I need to mention that later on, I would be accused in an email by Madhusudan of having fled the room during the interview without returning.)

On 15th April, I felt compelled to write an email

to Madhusudan to express my dismay that during his visit on 11th April, I had only managed to snatch a few minutes with him, with no proper guidance about Sai Grace Ashram, reminding him that he had written to me to say that the visit to Sai Grace was solely for my benefit and everything else was incidental.

On 17th April, Madhusudan wrote back to say that I should not have had any expectations. I was dumbfounded by his reply and wrote back that I would have to go into deep introspection due to his reply, as it was not an expectation I'd had, but a promise from him, that his visit was to discuss the future of Sai Grace Ashram and everything else was incidental.

On 24th April, I received another email from Madhusudan with an apology for his shortcomings.

On 25th April, I wrote to Madhusudan to say that I had heard the 24-minute YouTube announcement from Mr Chakravarthi from Sri Sathya Sai Central Trust at Prasanthi Nilayam, disclaiming Madhusudan as a fraud, as well as Narasimha Murthy. I offered to write to Mr Chakravarthi, whom I greatly admired, having had personal dealings with him over the years, to explain about all the amazing work being done out of Muddenahalli, with the guidance of Sai Baba through Madhusudan.

Madhusudan wrote back and gave his blessings

for me to do so. It felt good and right for me to defend him. I wrote a long email to Mr Chakravarthi, the draft okayed by Madhusudan.

I did not get a reply from Mr Chakravarthi.

On 28th April, I got an email from Madhusudan to say we needed to look for a house with at least 15-20 acres of land between exit 15-16 on the A12.

On 1st July, I flew back to Muddenahalli for Guru Poornima, the festival to honour the Guru. This was when Madhusudan told a friend of mine during darshan that no more improvements were to take place at Sai Grace. I wrote to Madhusudan saying I would have preferred if he had told me himself. This produced another Interview on my last day in Muddenahalli. We discussed again that I should continue setting up Sai Grace Trust to get charity status. This way we could register the new Ashram in the Sai Grace Trust once the right property had been found, as it was not in the London Trust Constitution to run and maintain a Spiritual Retreat Centre.

On 2nd August, Madhusudan wrote to say that my friend, Nila, could become one of my Trustees.

On 15th October, Madhusudan wrote to ask me to write a bit about how I came to Sri Sathya Sai Baba and consequently came to be in Muddenahalli, as he was writing his second book of the series, *The Story Divine*.

Once it was published, I note that he wrote: "Though she is happy to do her bit for her Lord and waits with bated breath for the next command, it is not easy by any stretch of the imagination for a lone lady to maintain Sai Grace all mostly by herself. Yet no delays or denials deter her dedication to her Master, as she lovingly tends to His devotees, who visit this Temple of healing from all over the world, to witness and experience the Divine love, which often manifests as showers of Vibhuti from the photos and other articles adorning the Ashram. While the journey has not always been easy, she has loved to learn the uncertainties of God and to carry on regardless."

On 19th October, I was back in Muddenahalli for Deepavali, the special Indian festival of Light. I just can't get enough of this holy place. I feel part of a big family, a feeling I have not had since a young child. There is always such joy in my heart when I am there.

On 1st December, I got invited to go to Rishikesh in the Himalayas. A magical trip, but no Interview was forthcoming. Unfortunately, I went down with flu so could not attend most of the events. But on the last day, I was urged by KR to attend the final Satsang, as Madhusudan was giving out a miniature Bhagavad-Gita to everyone present. KR said he would make sure a heater would be placed at the back of the hall to keep me warm, and I was to sit there. Madhusudan had asked Bhuvana to buy 120 of the miniature Bhagavad-Gita. As I was sitting right at the back of the Hall, I could see that more than 120 people were present, therefore I was not sure I would receive one. Slowly, Madhusudan walked past everyone, giving them the holy book. After reaching the end of the hall, he stood in front of me and looked at me with great concern. He touched my throat and said, "Fever. But you will be all right for travel tomorrow." With that, he produced one of the miniature Bhagavad-Gita. Later, I was told that 100 of the little holy books must have materialized, as there were close to 250 people present.

On 4th December, I received a loving email from Madhusudan to say that Swami sends His love and was sorry He could not see me for Interview in Rishikesh, but to look after myself.

On 7th February 2018, I was again back in my home-from-home in Muddenahalli for Shivaratri. I am a great fan of Shiva and totally excited about this boon. This was when a huge miracle happened; Madhusudan brought up a gold lingam from his mouth. Shortly after, he passed where I was sitting in first line and let me touch it. A very holy moment (I have a picture of this). On 11th February, I was asked to do Arati on stage in front of Sai Baba's empty chair; so sweet, as

I had prayed that KR would be able to do it as it was his birthday, but he had been called away on urgent business in Bangalore, so I ended up doing it for him!

On April 3rd 2018, Madhusudan and his entourage were coming back to Sai Grace Ashram for another visit. The event was a private one for forty people. I was extremely busy, getting all the preparations ready for their arrival. One month before they came, I slipped in the garden on some ice and injured my right knee. For some reason, I did not want to go to the hospital. Instead, I prayed intensely to Sai Baba to heal my knee in time for the big event. One week later, I fell again, because of the intense pain and weakened state of my leg and injured my right wrist. Truly it was an excruciating time for me. I was hobbling around, praying like mad that I would be all right on the day of the big arrival. My daily mantra was "Sai Baba, You are my doctor, You are my healer. Please heal me."

The day arrived. As Madhusudan got out of the car, he came straight to where I was standing by the front door to greet him. From nowhere, Vibhuti came out of his hand, which he so tenderly rubbed on my injured wrist. We had a divine Satsang in the Temple for forty people, followed by a delicious lunch.

Late afternoon, Madhusudan came down from his room and we had an evening Satsang in the sitting room, where the forty people had gathered. Sonja Venturi was there as well, singing devotional songs, in between talks and discourses being given by some of the entourage and myself. One particular talk was memorable, when dear Mr C Sreenivas told us that he had been in Sai Baba's hospital room, just before He had passed away. Sri Sreenivas was the only person in the room and was standing at the foot of the bed crying. When Sreenivas had first met Madhusudan in 2011 in Muddenahalli, Madhusudan had told him this story, which was personal, which convinced him that Madhusudan was indeed being channelled by Sai Baba. Sri Sreenivas was the spearhead in getting the three Children Heart Hospitals constructed. He was incidentally also the C Sreenivas who had signed the note for me to get into the VIP section of Sai Baba's Ashram on my first visit in 1994. What a coincidence! As Madhusudan retired for the night, but before he went up the stairs, he told me it was one of the most relaxed and happy times he'd had in a foreign Ashram.

Next morning was Good Friday. Madhusudan had asked me to prepare an Easter service, which even he was moved by. We have some truly beautiful pictures taken by Gabriella Campomizzi, who had been taking photos of Sai Baba for thirty-five years, which are now in my albums to be treasured forever.

On 13th April, I got an email from Madhusudan to express thanks for the Divine visit and to take care of myself.

Mid-April was to be the Inauguration of the Italian Ashram in Assisi. I was invited to go. My leg and wrist were still painful, but I decided that I would get on the plane anyway and fly to Assisi. It was a blessed time being part of the celebrations of the new Italian Ashram. After the evening Satsang, Madhusudan came up to me and asked if I had been shown around the Ashram. I told him "No," so he said he would show me himself. There was a narrow winding stone staircase leading to the second floor with a banister on the right side, which I looked at thinking it would be impossible for me to climb, with my leg and arm still very painful, plus waring a saree. The next think I knew, I was standing next to Madhusudan at the top of the stairs!

The following day, friends were getting a bit concerned that I was still limping and in considerable pain.

It was arranged for me to have some x-rays taken at a local private clinic. We arrived there and first my wrist was x-rayed. The doctor duly came out, showing us the results, that indicated my wrist was broken but had a perfect break with all the tiny bones in alignment. Then it was decided that I was to have my knee scanned, and the same thing happened; a break all around the knee was revealed, but all the small fragments in perfect alignment! The doctors were truly amazed that for two months I had been walking on a broken leg, as well as a broken wrist, but had never had a cast put on either break. They looked pretty dumbfounded and asked my friends who I was! How could I explain that it was without a doubt Sai Baba who had manifested the healing to take place as I had put such faith in Him? That He was my doctor and my healer.

On 1st May, a brochure of a beautiful property arrived through the letterbox at Sai Grace. Madhusudan had expressed a wish to halt the search for the new Sai Grace Ashram, as he wanted the payment to be paid off for the Hostel at the Mandya school in India by the London Trust. But something made me send the details to Madhusudan anyway. He immediately wrote back and said to bring the brochure to Kodaikanal in May. What an honour to be asked to come back to this holy place.

On the 3rd May, 100 students and 150 guests were invited to Kodaikanal. In the mornings, we would all gather in the newly constructed Temple down a small recline, in a serene setting of the woods. In the early evening, we would gather at the main Hilltop Ashram and have beautiful discourses, including musical recitals. Truly a blessed time was had by all.

As the last day was almost at an end and I had not been granted an Interview, I started wondering what was going on. As I had been suffering from a dreadful stomach bug for the past few days, felt weak and tired, I decided I wanted to leave and go back to my hotel room. I went to say goodbye to some friends when I bumped into KR. He urged me to stay for a while as he said 'Swami' was coming soon on his way to the dining room. A long line of devotees had started to form along the walls leading down to the dining room, so I decided to join them. I saw KR standing opposite me, with one of my girlfriends standing next to me, trying to hold me up, as I was feeling very weak.

As Madhusudan came out, he walked passed me, and as he did, I shouted out from the depth of my being, "Goodbye, Swami."

There was suddenly an almighty hush. I saw KR visibly paling beneath his tan, and my girlfriend holding onto me started shaking.

Madhusudan swivelled round and looked at me in surprise. In his sweet voice he said, "Are you not coming to have something to eat?"

I said, "No, Swami, I have been sick and not feeling inclined to eat."

He said, "Well, I am going to have some food now and then I will see you afterwards. Go and wait for me."

About 30 minutes later, I was asked to go up to the Interview room. As I entered the room, I was surprised to see sitting there the Trustees of the London Trust. Madhusudan told everyone present how delighted Sai Baba was about the property I had brought for His attention to become the new UK Ashram and instructed me to go back and make a bid to purchase it. He also said that I would be in charge of the new Ashram and living there full time. He asked the Trustees to be as supportive as possible to me, as that had not always been the case! All the Trustees agreed to help me in any way they could. One Trustee in particular was tearful, asking to be forgiven, for maybe not having been as supportive as he should have been, but said he would mend his ways!

On my return to the UK, I went directly from Heathrow to see the new property to put in an offer. It was such a perfect house, with twelve bedrooms, nine bathrooms and a huge kitchen, as well as a smaller one. There were also three magnificent barns, ready to be renovated into further accommodation. It was our intention to turn this beautiful place, set in nearly 15 acres, surrounded by 300 acres of farmland, into a Centre for Human Excellence and the place where Prema Sai would come and live one month a year when He started to do His world travels. And it was not expensive for what it had to offer!

Shortly, another bit of Karma would work its way out, when I would be stabbed in the back by a certain person, who was complaining to anyone willing to listen, as to why I had put this new project in front of Madhusudan, as this person thought it was much too expensive to buy. This is recorded in a strong-worded email he wrote to me on 24th May, which I forward to Madhusudan for him to digest.

On 25th May, I got an email from Madhusudan to say that if we couldn't get the new property for £1.5 million, then I should look for another property.

It took me twelve months to negotiate with the Estate Agent various points to bring down the price, get ownership of the road leading up to the gates of the property and get a bit more land to the East to square off the property, which would also allow for the farmer to take a different route when he would start farming the surrounding land.

On 19th June, Madhusudan wrote to say that he would like his right-hand lady, Bhuvana, to become my second Trustee.

On 19th July, I was back in Muddenahalli. On my last day, I got an Interview, with Bhuvana also in attendance, to talk about Sai Grace Trust. It was decided that as soon as we had charity status, the new property should be purchased in the new Trust's name to avoid stamp duty.

On 9th September, Bhuvana came to visit me in Sai Grace. I took her to see the new property. She also fell in love with this beautiful place and thought it would make an ideal Prema Sai Ashram, a Centre for Human Excellence.

At the end of November, I got another invitation to Rishikesh in the Himalayas and stayed again in Parmarth Niketan Ashram by the Ganga River. How grateful I am that I could be part of the group who was chosen to go. I felt as if I had lived by the Ganga River in a previous life and would be so happy to be back there again, breathing in the holy energy and past memories.

I flew via Mumbai, where we were to inaugurate the 2nd Children Heart Hospital. Having lifted a heavy suitcase at the airport, I gave myself a back injury, with a hairline fracture in the lower part of my spine. I was in total agony, and only by a miracle, a few days later, having been treated by several doctors who were in our group, got to Parmarth Niketan Ashram and collapsed on my bed. By sheer luck, there was a clinic just yards from my room that specialised in spine injuries. Twice a day, I would go there for treatments.

I managed to hobble down to the Ganga River to look at a shop there that specialized in holy statues, in the view to get a couple for the apartment Madhusudan was staying in. I chose three beautiful statues. KR happened to be just walking by the shop, so together we brought them back to Madhusudan's apartment.

At the end of my stay, I got an Interview, with Bhuvana who was also present. We spoke about the property for the new Ashram. We went into great detail about all I had managed to negotiate with the estate agent back in the UK. Madhusudan told me that by June of the next year, the place would be purchased and I was to settle there to look after it. My home, Moat Hall, would be sold after this date, and the money from the sale could help maintain the new property and the outbuildings to be renovated. He told me that he would come in April the following year and I was to get a viewing ready for him and his entourage. He also told me that he was arranging help with the finances for the new Ashram, but to up the offer to £1.6 million to keep the owners happy (all recorded on my phone).

At the end of the Interview, I asked Madhusudan to clarify the constitution for the renewed effort in getting Charity Status for Sai Grace Trust. He said, "Don't mention Sai Baba's name, it is too complicated. It will not happen if you do."

As the Interview came to an end, Madhusudan told me he had enjoyed the holy statues of Shiva,

Ganesh and the Shiva family I had brought for him and that I was to take them back to Sai Grace Ashram and place them in Sai Baba's bedroom.

Back in the UK, I had many problems trying to keep the estate agent confident that we were serious about buying the property. Little did they know that I was having problems finding the finances! Nobody seemed willing to help with the purchase of this beautiful, perfect property. Over the preceding months, I was writing back and forth to Madhusudan to say we had to show the owners of the property that money was in the bank to put down a deposit once we'd had a survey done. We got one letter of intent from a devotee of £500,000 and a further promise from the head of the London Trust of £500,000. This was still a shortfall of £600,000. It was an extremely stressful time for me, wondering how we were going to get the full sum for the purchase.

On 10th December, Madhusudan asked a rich girlfriend of mine to send me £160,000 for a deposit on the new property, which duly arrived in Sai Grace Trust bank account on 12th December.

During this time, I was also having problems getting Charity Status from the Charity Commission. Eventually, I decided to hire an expensive lawyer, conversed in Charity law. She told me that I needed to write in the Constitution that the Sai Grace Trust would teach the ancient art of Meditation and Yoga, as well as the teachings of Sri Sathya Sai Baba. This I then did without consulting Madhusudan, because the past two application attempts had failed with his advice of not mentioning Sai Baba's name.

March 2019, I found myself in Muddenahalli for Shivarathri again. I just loved being in my beautiful flat and amongst my Sai family. I could easily stay there indefinitely. This time, Madhusudan brought up two gold lingams. Such Divine blessings for everyone.

On 3rd April 2019, Madhusudan and his entourage arrived from India. I met them at the new property, with all the trustees from the London Trust, as well as their wives. The estate agent representative was an angel and turned a blind eye to all these people turning up. I spent 55 minutes walking around the property with Madhusudan recording his impressions; he fell in love with the place. When we walked into the huge master bedroom, he turned to my girlfriend who had sent the deposit for the new Ashram and said, "How would you like this as your bedroom?" We all burst out laughing, as we thought this a huge joke.

That evening, we all gathered at the London Trust Chair's house for evening dinner and Satsang. It was there a huge bomb shell was dropped on me, when

Madhusudan announced that my girlfriend was going to donate all the money to buy the new property. I was mystified, as I had not been told this. In fact, I was so taken aback that I left and went back to my hotel room to mull over the insensitive way this new turn of events had been dealt with.

Next morning, I went back to the Chair's house and was called in for an Interview with Madhusudan, accompanied by my Trustees he had chosen for Sai Grace Trust, his right-hand lady, Bhuvana, and dear Nila. He told me it would take a long time for me to get Charity Status for Sai Grace Trust, therefore asking my girlfriend to purchase the new Ashram property was the way forward, as I still had not managed to get Sai Grace Trust registered with the Charity Commission. I tried to tell him that it was imminent, that I would get the covered status, but he was adamant. He also mentioned that later my girlfriend would gift the property to Sai Grace Trust, after she had lived in the new Ashram for a year. I believe now he only told me that to keep me quiet.

On 12th April, I was asked to return the £160,000 sent by my girlfriend into the Sai Grace Trust bank account as the deposit for the new Ashram. I immediately did so.

Three weeks later on 3rd May 2019, I got the

wonderful news that I had received Charity Status for Sai Grace Trust CIO! What a blessed day that was. I sent the news via email to Madhusudan, and he wrote back, "That was quick." No congratulations or anything to that effect. Even my girlfriend started blanking me and would not let me have anything to do with the new Ashram purchase.

Many months later, I found out from my girlfriend, who had by then had had a falling out with Madhusudan, that he had announced to all and sundry at the London Chair's house that I would *never* get Charity Status.

A week later, I was on my way to Kodaikanal for a three-day visit, but I was not invited in for Interview. As my trustee, Bhuvana, was not there, I anticipated that I would get an Interview that would include her, once I was back in Muddenahalli a few days later.

At the last Satsang in the Temple, a strange thing happened. It had been a divine, magical morning, and the atmosphere in the Temple was serene and peaceful. As Madhusudan came walking down the middle of the Temple on his way out, he passed a lady around 30 years of age, sitting on the floor, flanking the red carpet. She handed him a note, which he proceeded to read. He must have passed on a few feet, when suddenly he swivelled around, ripped the note into pieces and threw them at her, shouting, "How dare she say I only give Interview to rich people?"

There was a stunned silence everywhere, as Madhusudan proceeded to exit the Temple. I could see people sitting around the young lady slowly melt away; her head was bowed down in tears. No one approached her, they seemed not to want to be near her. I sat waiting, inwardly asking my Sai Baba if I should go to her and say something. I got a firm, "Yes, do."

I went up to the young lady and bent down, putting my arm around her, saying to her that I was a Minister and just wanted to support her in her obvious pain. I felt the tenseness in her body through her clothes. She was shaking and tears were streaming down her cheeks. After a few minutes, she said, "I don't know why I wrote that." I told her she had probably been used as an instrument, to be brave and try to understand why she had done that. Maybe all it would take to make things right was to write another note, explaining why she had written what she had. We sat silently for a few more minutes. Slowly, I felt her body and mind relax. For me, it was my duty to comfort this lady, who had been so bitterly insulted by her Guru in front of everyone. In fact, this kind of incident could produce any kind of harmful aftereffect from her turbulent mind.

Shortly, we were asked to leave the Temple by a

couple of people, who were trying to close it up. There was a big outdoor event in the Ashram gardens, which had already started, so I told the lady I would accompany her to go up there. She said she would wait a while by herself to collect her thoughts. I was worried for her but had no choice but to leave her alone. As I climbed the stairs leading up to the Ashram, I kept praying that Sai Baba would comfort her and take care of her.

As I got to the garden gate, KR came rushing up to me, asking me where I had been, as the event had started, but a seat had been kept for me near Madhusudan. I sat down and just stared at him. He quietly stared back at me, but I could see the incident had affected him. There was almost a sadness about him. It took ages for me to concentrate on the fun everyone was having, but slowly I saw Madhusudan relax as well. Inwardly, I asked him to forgive me for having to fulfil my duty as a Minister, that I had not meant to disrespect his actions, if that had been what was needed for the young lady concerned.

Later, I learnt that Madhusudan had arranged for the young lady and her fiancé, who was working at Muddenahalli Ashram, to have a beautiful wedding paid for by the Ashram Trust. The reason she had written the note was because she had desperately wanted an Interview with Madhusudan, as her parents were apparently not in favour of her marriage and were giving her a hard time.

We have to be so careful before we judge people, as often we do not know the full story.

I travelled back to Muddenahalli, but after four days of being totally ignored, I wrote to Madhusudan to say I was leaving the next morning and would like to hand him the Sai Grace Trust CIO papers that I had brought for him. He wrote back, "Bring to darshan tomorrow." This I did. At the very last second, before he left the Temple Hall, he came by me and took the Sai Grace Trust papers and just said, "That was quick," with not another word. I felt cold all over, as his attitude was like a cold shower descending upon me.

In June, Bhuvana wrote to me to say that she and the Chair of the London Trust would be handling the inauguration of the new property, which would probably be the 2nd or 3rd week in October.

When Bhuvana held her Sai Youth conference on 25th September, she said there were only two Ashrams in Europe, namely Turkey and Italy - no mention of the one in UK? She also said that it was now mandatory to attend at least four visits per year to Sai Youth Conferences around the world! I got calls from many Sai devotees to ask me, "How does she think they can afford that, as well as all the donations they are giving to Muddenahalli? And why is Sai Grace Ashram being blanked?" I told them I was as bewildered as they were.

On 21st October, I wrote to Madhusudan asking for clarification, as there seemed to be no interest in Sai Grace Ashram from the moment I had got charity status. I got a reply back from him the next day saying that he had been led to believe that not all was well at Sai Grace, as I had been heard talking badly about him. He went further to say that it would probably be best if I went independent, under my own ample leadership, and that I was free to do what I wanted, without Swami's help!

What! Just like that, dumped unceremoniously? I was in shock. I wrote back and said, "Have you ever heard the saying 'Beware of the student who whispers poison in the teacher's ear for his/her own benefit?' I wrote that, yes, I had mentioned to just a very few people that, since Guru Poornima festival in July, I had been unhappy about the fact that he was sitting in the designated Chair for Sai Baba, announcing on that day to the world that he was now fully operating as Sai Baba.

I also wrote that I still held him in high esteem, as I believed 100% that he was being *guided* by Sri Sathya Sai Baba.

It seemed inconceivable that Madhusudan, on his own, could find the devotees to pay for the twenty-two schools that had been built, all free of cost to the students attending a superb education, as well as the three Children Heart Hospitals, without a bill counter, which were up and running by now, all built in nine months, which was a trait of Sathya Sai Baba.

Not to mention the University for Human Excellence, as well as the Annapoorna breakfast program, feeding over a million children a healthy breakfast every morning.

But Madhusudan's *inconsistency* in what he wrote in his following two emails in relation to me was to be questioned. He went even further to say that he had never wanted my home as the UK Ashram anyway! It was full of untruths, as well as defamation of my reputation and character. I still have all the emails he has written to me, as well as the recordings during interviews. But how hurtful it was, to have my gift to God thrown back into my face so unceremoniously.

My last email to him on the above was that it was a good thing I was a strong person, trying to practice non-attachment, otherwise it might be a case of wanting to cut one's wrists. How nice it would have been if this supposedly God-risen person had confronted me in person so we could have talked out what was bothering him. Sai Baba used to say, "If you have doubts or questions, ask me and I will answer."

So, with sadness in my heart, we parted ways. I

realized how fond I had become of Madhusudan, as well as all the tender-hearted people I had met through the Sai Mission out of Muddenahalli, apart from a few, whom I now know to have been partly instrumental in poisoning me to Madhusudan. Gossip is an assignation by the coward.

But most importantly, I have understood that my Sathya Sai Baba would never allow anything to happen to me, if it was not but for my highest good, otherwise it simply would not have happened. We never know what is best for us, but Sai Baba always knows what is best for us and will always only give us that. If we believe we are in a situation that we think is not favourable, it is only a misunderstanding. Sai Baba will never put us in a situation that is unfavourable for us. He loves us too much. So I must believe that I had to have this experience. In that knowledge, how can I condemn Madhusudan or anyone else from Muddenahalli in playing out the drama that unfolded and then collapsed? I am instructed to just send them LOVE.

It took me a while to get used to the idea that I was no longer to be part of Muddenahalli and all it implied. I realized I had become engrossed in this special Ashram, the special people who were part of this holy place, as well as the honour of having been chosen to hold the space for the UK Prema Sai Ashram.

I felt as if they had become a loving family, but now they were gone. The **twelfth step in going BEYOND FORGIVENESS.**

However, with endless gratitude to all concerned, I give thanks for the incredible experiences I had whilst being involved with Muddenahalli. Before the breakdown, I had gathered some unforgettable memories, travels and lessons, which I might otherwise never have undertaken.

Sonja at the piano for Inauguration 2016 of Sai Grace Ashram.

Madhusudan Sai kneeling at Baba's Chair without cushion!

2018 Madhusudan Sai making Vibhuti for me

Showing my father's cross

Event for 250 people 2017

Sai Baba's chair with cushion!

All photos of Sadguru Madhusudan Sai have been given consent by him to be published. The photos have been taken by Gabriella Campomizzi

THE MEANING OF FORGIVENESS

I told you that something might come again and tap me on the shoulder to ask if I truly and finally had under control **forgiveness at the deepest level.**

Going BEYOND FORGIVENESS means falling into an ocean where there is only pure love. This is where you can survive at your optimal best, to reach your highest potential and create a life that is worth living and remembering, as well as understanding that all there is, is Love.

Instead, I stayed at Moat Hall, running Sai Grace the best way I could through counselling people over the phone and holding services for a few people at a time, as well as memorial services. I also opened up a YouTube channel, *Reverend Leonora van Gils,* recording a few Meditations and Prayers to be of help during the difficult times. The music for them was composed by my dear loyal friend Sonja Venturi, who has also written and composed a beautiful song for *Beyond Forgiveness.* You can listen to it on www.beyondforgiveness.co.uk. Over the years, she has been of tremendous support and strength, through thick and thin, as I believe I have been of great support to her as well.

During the Coronavirus lockdown, I was happy

and content in myself to go ever deeper within, to connect with the eternal me that is beyond the illusions of this body. Stepping ever deeper into silence is my great salvation. It seems that all of life's ups and downs have afforded me the luxury of arriving in this blissful state, of being self-contained and happy in my own company.

EPILOGUE

I recently received an email from Madhusudan, asking me if I would be willing to give up my flat in Muddenahalli so that a teacher couple at the school there could call it their home, as they were living outside the Ashram. I wrote back that I had no problem with that and it was my pleasure. It was of course a bit of a wrench to give up my home-from-home, but all my belongings from there were lovingly passed on to KR, who distributed them to whomever he felt would like them.

END OF 2021.

It is interesting that the idea of Sai Baba having taken over Madhusudan is supposedly no longer so, told in his own words during a discourse delivered in Muddenahalli this year, but that he is now Sadguru Sri Madhusudan Sai in his own right. Apparently, by his own efforts, he has raised himself up to become a Guru, whereas Sai Baba was born an Avatar (a Divine incarnation of the highest, with all His faculties in place). I have absolutely no problem with Madhusudan Sai becoming a Guru through his own efforts, as I believe we can all elevate ourselves into High Beings. I still believe that he is being guided by Sai Baba and trying his best to move the Sai Mission forward to its conclusion. But we must remember, so are other amazing Sai Missions that are happening around the world, in silent service!

I had to spend some time in understanding and thereby forgiving Madhusudan Sai for the way he had behaved towards me, when it seemed I was unable to find the finances for the new Ashram. He was maybe also annoyed that I had put in the Constitution of Sai Grace Trust CIO that the teachings of Sri Sathya Sai Baba were part of the Objects, when he had asked me not to.

I remember during my last visit to Muddenahalli, I told KR what a failure I felt that I had not managed to find the finances for the new Ashram and how bewildered I felt in the way Madhusudan was treating me. His last words to me were, "You must forgive him."

And so another big lesson in forgiveness and detachment. I would not have missed it for the world. We cannot change the past, but we can carve a new future with no regrets. We hold the key to our own freedom. Freedom lies in learning to embrace what happened. Victimhood comes from the inside. No one can make you a victim but you yourself. After pouring salt into wounds, it manages to drag out more memories; we are not that which confounds us.

Sadguru Sri Madhusudan Sai, you will always have a special place in my heart. Thank you for the time we spent together, for the lessons, as well as the love I experienced from you, until you decided to withdraw it.

Your biggest mistake is doing something for someone and expecting something in return. If you don't get anything in return, you can become resentful, which destroys the deed in the first place. This is something I have tried to practice all my life; to give and not expect anything in return.

~~~~~~~~~~~~~~~~~~~~~~

So what now? I think we are learning to bridge a new way of existing, all of us who have used this opportunity of lockdown to look deeper into who we are, how far we have come in this interesting holy journey we are on. We have maybe even come up with the answer that we are 'Lighter' and more 'Conscious' of this wonderful opportunity of knowing our true self. What if these unprecedented times have actually been an invitation to listen more deeply to our own silent souls, witnessing a deeper meaning of why we are here, having taken this spiritual journey into healing?

"The word 'healing' is related to the word 'holy'. Healing is the return of the memory of wholeness. When you are whole, you are holy and you are healed. When you are whole, you also lose the fear of death, because you recognize that death is a creative opportunity to recreate yourself. So the secret to healing is actually the secret to Enlightenment.

Enlightenment means going beyond your ego-encapsulated self and becoming self-aware" (words by Deepak Chopra).

It is your destiny to see as God
sees, and feel as God feels.
We have to ask ourselves,
What will it take for us to realize
that we too are God?

The other night I had a beautiful dream of Sai Baba. He was lying in state in a small room. One by one, people were allowed to come and spend a few minutes by His side. When it was my turn, I knelt by His bed, when to my amazement, He slowly opened

His eyes, raised Himself up, widening His arms, then wrapped them around me. As He did so, I felt a rush of His endless Love as He whispered in my ear, "You are always so loyal to me."

CONCLUSION

And so it is January 2022 and I have just moved from precious Moat Hall. This in itself was an extraordinary ordeal. Mid-2021, I found a buyer, who are devout Buddhists and have made a beautiful job of the garden, and thus the holy energy which was built up over the sixteen years I was there will go on and on. But the estate agent made a big hash of handling the sale, and I lost a lot of money in the end, but like all things that are disturbing and unfair, I have chosen to put it down as an unfortunate experience.

But Sai Baba was ever kind to arrange for me to have practiced detachment for so long, allowing His will to work through me, so I would not find it too difficult to leave this beautiful Sai Spiritual Healing Centre behind, with all its amazing memories and miracles placed in my heart, as well as hundreds of other people's hearts, in safety forever.

I have moved into an adorable little, cosy, warm house in the village of Darsham. It is a perfect house inside, with a sweet little manageable garden. Here I have no worries and live in peaceful silence, but still with some nice people close by. Now I can peacefully continue my work for the Charity, Sai Grace Trust CIO. I love counselling people over the phone and try helping as many people as possible. I am amazed how I still get endless calls from the Interview I did in 2008 for Jody and Ted Henry on their YouTube channel *Souljourn*.

I am determined to finish my book and get it published. I think it has a lot to offer anyone who has had a dramatic life but is looking for **understanding, peace and salvation**; that is my object, that is my prayer.

Without understanding why things happen to us, we have no hope of finding peace.

If I have this grace I am living now instead of my biological father's love, I would not trade it for the world. The love I experienced from my Eternal Father is enough to sustain me forever.

12 STEPS TOWARDS GOING BEYOND FORGIVENESS

How necessary is forgiveness to living our best life?

First of all, I believe it is necessary to feel the hurt, the sorrow, the anger, the despair, the abuse, the abandonment of violated boundaries before it can all pass into Love. The part of you that has felt all the above has to be validated to be able to drench those parts of yourself in forgiveness, the parts that have made you feel worthless and not able to live the grandest vision of who you truly are. How do you do that if you have no prior knowledge of how to cope or have no mentor who can guide you back on the path you came here to walk on towards your highest goal that will bring you Home?

If we open our heart to ourself, we may be able to open our heart to the one who hurt us. Without condoning what they did, without making excuses for their unconscious behaviors, we may be able to find compassion in time, see the unloved part of them that just did not know how to live or love or behave.

Do not shame yourself in any way if you are unable to forgive right away. Do not call yourself weak or a coward; you are neither. Forgiveness can happen at any time as you drop into the depths of yourself and find the essential *you* that can never be taken away from you. Forgiveness is primarily self-forgiveness.

For some miraculous reason, I managed to go through what I had to endure as a child and come out of it without it having disturbed my mental health. But I believe I am a rare case. As one psychiatrist once told me many years ago, "Leonora, you are walking medical history. You should in fact be totally screwed up, but you are not; you are one of the healthiest people I have had the pleasure to meet."

In later years, I have been able to work on myself through self-help books and then of course the ultimate bonus of meeting the great Avatar Sri Sathya Sai Baba, who took me under His Divine wings in a subtle way that lead me to salvation of knowing who I truly am.

This is why I now must pay Him back for His Love He bestowed on me, trusting me enough to bring His Message of love through this book.

I was asking myself this question last night before I went to bed: Is it necessary to put my story out there? Please give me a sign, dear Beloved Sai.

I opened up my iPhone and searched the YouTube channel of Aravind Balasubramanya, who is a special ex-student of Sai Baba and has recorded hundreds of divine stories of his time with the Avatar. Low and behold, the following story jumped out at me:

WHY SHARE PERSONAL EXPERIENCES? AND HOW?

Aravind starts off by saying, "Is a personal experience meant to be shared or not? A personal experience belongs to the innermost recess of your heart. It is up to you if you want to share it or not. It is in your hands if you want to share it or not." He prayed to Sai to give him a sign if it was all right for him to share all the personal stories and experiences he'd had the grace to have with Sai when He was with us in body. The answer came through a book he was reading, *The Lives of Saints,* written by Swami Shivananda.

Swami Shivananda had met Sai Baba and been cured by Him from a problem he'd had with his knees, leaving him unable to walk. In this book, there is a story of a disciple who wanted a mantra from his Guru, as he had not been accepted as a full disciple but wanted to get in touch with that position. He had to go eighteen times to get initiated into a mantra for Enlightenment. On the nineteenth visit, the Guru relented but told him that it was "of the utmost importance for him to keep it to himself and never tell anyone of this secret mantra. He must surely not give it to anyone who was not worthy, but I have found you worthy now and that is why I am willing to share it with you."

So it was, the disciple was given the mantra, "Om Nama Narayana." How we know this, as it was such a secret, is because as soon as it was told, the disciple ran up to the top of the temple and shouted to all the people below, "All of you, listen! Here is the pathway to liberation!" He started shouting, "Om Namo Narayana! But remember, while uttering these words, you must surrender yourself fully to God. You will then surely get liberation."

He did this despite the warning from his Guru not to share the mantra he had been given. His Guru had also said to him that if he did divulge the secret mantra, he would have to suffer in hell for a thousand lifetimes.

People came running to the Guru to say what had happened. He summoned the disciple who had been so disobedient. He came, fell at his Guru's feet, and said, "I don't mind going to hell a thousand times if this mantra can help the spiritual progress for a thousand people. Forgive me and punish me in whatever way. I am ready." The Guru had tears in his eyes because the selflessness of the disciple had touched him. He said, "You have to listen to what I have to say. I hereby appoint you as my successor." This was the story Aravind came across when he inwardly asked Sai if he should share his personal stories about Him or not.

Aravind continues to say, "But we have to use the four filters before we speak or write if it helps people to feel closer to the message of the story:

1. Is it true?
2. Will it hurt anyone?
3. Have you recalled and researched every aspect of the story, with no exaggerations?
4. Will it inflate your ego?

My answer to these filters:

1a) I have tried very hard to be totally truthful in telling my story.

2a) I hope it has not hurt anyone, but if it has, I am so sorry, but it was essential to be truthful.

3a) I have done thorough recall and research of every aspect of my story and tried my best not to exaggerate anything. The Muddenahalli story can be backed up by all emails and recordings.

4a) For sure I have not written this story to inflate my ego. In fact, it has been extremely hard to write about the early part of my life and as an adult. I am not particularly proud of some of the things I had to go through, although most of them were not of my own doing, but some of them were. Am I waiting for an apology for anyone who inflicted pain, lies and deceit upon me? No is the answer, precisely because I have learnt to go BEYOND FORGIVENESS. Therein lies the need of no apology.

Instead of going into deep pain and confusion every time a new drama presented itself to me during my life, I began to realize that my suffering is not who I am, it is just a byproduct of who I AM.

Let me therefore turn this book into a positive gift to humanity, for anyone reading it, so they too can discover who they are, as it will sustain them for eternity.

The TRUTH lies within you, as does the power you will ever need to change the direction of your life; you can tap into that power whenever you wish.

When we have a shift in consciousness, everything changes. Self- repair comes into play and reveals our true identity: self-regulation and self-repair is healing. The way you think changes the power of intention, then becomes greater. There is more freedom in choice, more creativity. We also find ourselves experiencing compassion, joy, equanimity, loving kindness and, most importantly, peace of mind, as we get in touch with that part of ourselves that is inseparable from all that exists.

You will never truly know the daily struggle of others. The courage it took them to leave behind what was not for them, is also the courage that will help them find what *is* for them.

I hope by sharing, it will bring more humility into my life, with a knowing that it was maybe unavoidable to tell it, as it just might be of some help to even just one person out there.

Maybe your life purpose isn't supposed to be a life thrilling narrative? What if you are meant to be the sunshine in someone's stormy day? Or the voice of clarity to a frantic mind? You don't have to be a superhero to save the world.

Out beyond ideas of right doing and wrong doing, there is a field. I will meet you there. (Rumi)

THE LAW OF SURRENDER AND DETATCHMENT

Surrender opens the door to the miraculous.

Many people equate attachment with love.

Attachment deprives us of love.

*Attachment comes from fear, and
fear is the opposite of love.*

Attachment is always exclusive, and love is inclusive.

Attachment is bondage and love is freedom.

Attachment is demanding and love imposes no demands.

Attachment always seeks control.

*Non-attachment is a state of freedom that
preserves and increases your love for another.*

*In true surrender, we never feel the need to control, or
convince, or bully, or manipulate, or insist, or beg, or
seduce, as we know how to allow, and in that allowing,
we invite love to create miracles.(Deepak Chopra)*

In the state of surrender and non-attachment, we need the following qualities:

No anger or fear.

We trust the universe is on our side.

We believe we are enough and good enough as we are.

We work on the tenderness and sweetness for the love of others.

We put our loving energy into every situation.

We know our own needs, without having to seek outside approval.

We cultivate the peace of inner silence.

We understand that nothing is ever lost, it is only transformed.

We form our desires from the depth of our heart and watch the higher self-carry them out.

It is not easy to ask for help. People who are victims of abuse need to talk to someone urgently. I did not have that opportunity, but by a miracle, I never gave up on myself.

I follow this mantra and now pass it on to you:

"I forgive everyone, including myself. I release the past with love and acceptance."

TOOLS FOR SELF-HELP

If you suffer from pain in your thumb ligament or wrist, the best help is to get a magnetic bracelet and wear it all the time. It gets rid of the pain in no time.

The Tapping Solution App is another way of helping yourself get over any trauma, insomnia, weight loss, etc.

A healthy diet is a must. I drink hot water and lemon every morning, followed by turmeric, Neem oil capsule and an Omega 3/6/7/9 capsule.

After the age of 50 onwards, take a good cranberry supplement every night; it is a fantastic insurance for never getting a urinary infection as you get older.

For men, eat pumpkin seed butter every morning and pumpkin seeds during the day, but chew them well! It is supposedly great for preventing prostate cancer.

MORE ON SAI BABA

"I have not come on any mission of publicity
for any sect or creed or cause.
Nor have I come to collect followers for any doctrine.
I have no plan to attract disciples
or devotees into My Fold.
I have come to tell you of this Unitary Faith
This Atmic Principle, this perfect Love
This duty to Love, this obligation to Love
I have come to inscribe a Golden Chapter
in the history of Humanity
Wherein falsehood will fail.
Truth will triumph and virtue will reign.
Character will confer power then,
Not knowledge in inventive skill, nor wealth."
(Bhagawan Sri Sathya Sai Baba)

Sai Baba has come to light the lamp of
love in your heart. He has not come
to gather devotees or start a new religion.
Sai Baba is the great reminder. He tells us over and
over again that we are human beings with the capacity
of having a divine experience of who we truly are.
God born, living in God and eventually going home
to God. That is why it is so important to find out that
our most worthwhile occupation is living in God, the
Truth which is ever permanent. We have to remind
ourselves that everything else is impermanent.

Nobody can force Sai Baba to enter someone's
heart, but we can soften their hearts by
telling our experiences of Him, so that when
He shows up, they will recognize Him.

You cannot believe in God until you believe in yourself.

MY VOWS AS AN INTER-FAITH MINISTER

1. *I vow to be truthful to myself and others.*
2. *I vow to accept the many paths to God.*
3. *I vow to serve wisely and with deep sincerity.*
4. *I vow never to destroy another's Faith. Even the
   simples Faith leads to God.*

After costs, some donations are going to the following Charities:

- Prashanthi Balamandira Trust
- Sri Sathya Sai Sanjeevani Children's Heart Hospitals
- Sri Sathya Sai Sarla Memorial Hospital in Muddenahalli
- Sai Fertility India
- A Light for Ukraine in collaboration with VsI Sai Prema Lithuania

References

Page 1 - Sreyan svadharmo vigunah paradharmat svanusthitat;

Svadharme nidhanam sreyah paradharmo bhayavahah (Chapter 3. Verse 35)

Meaning: It is better to follow one's own dharma through imperfection than the dharma of someone else, even though well-performed. Better is death in one's own dharma; another person's dharma is fraught with fear.

Page 1 - Geoffrey Francis Fisher, Baron Fisher of Lambeth, GCVO, PC (5 May 1887 – 15 September 1972) was an English Anglican priest and 99th Archbishop of

Canterbury, serving from 1945 to 1961. Fisher officiated at the marriage of Princess Elizabeth in Westminster Abbey in 1947, and after her accession to the throne, he led the coronation service in 1953 and crowned her as Queen.

Read here (https://en.wikipedia.org/wiki/Geoffrey_Fisher) how he also stopped Princess Margaret from marrying a divorced man.

BOOK COVER: PHOTO BY GABRIELLA CAMPOMIZZI